Fiorello La Guardia
Ethnicity and Reform

American Biographical History Series

Fiorello La Guardia
Ethnicity and Reform

Ronald H. Bayor
Georgia Institute of Technology

Harlan Davidson, Inc.
Wheeling, Illinois 60090-6000

Library of Congress Cataloging-in-Publication Data
Bayor, Ronald H., 1944–
    Fiorello H. La Guardia : ethnicity and reform / Ron-
ald H. Bayor.
        p.   cm.—(American biographical history series)
    Includes bibliographical references (p. 195) and in-
dex.
    ISBN 0-88295-894-1
    1. La Guardia, Fiorello H. (Fiorello Henry), 1882–
1947. 2. Legislators—United States—Biography. 3.
Mayors—New York (N.Y.)—Biography. 4. United
States. Congress. House—Biography. 5. New York
(N.Y.)—Politics and government—1898–1950. I. Title.
II. Series.
E748.L23B38   1992
974.7'1042'092—dc20   92-32970
[B]   CIP

Cover photo and frontispiece: The LaGuardia and
Wagner Archives, LaGuardia Community College / The
City University of New York.

Manufactured in the United States of America
98 97 96 95 94 2 3 4 5 6 MG

As biographies offer access to the past, they reflect the needs of the present. Newcomers to biography and biographical history often puzzle over the plethora of books that some lives inspire. "Why do we need so many biographies of Abraham Lincoln?" they ask, as they search for the "correct" version of the sixteenth president's story. Each generation needs to revisit Lincoln because each generation has fresh questions, inspired by its own experiences. Collectively, the answers to these questions expand our understanding of Lincoln and America in the 1860s, but they also assist us to better comprehend our own time. People concerned with preserving such civil liberties as freedom of the press in time of national crisis have looked at Lincoln's approach to political opposition during and after secession. Civil rights activists concerned with racial injustice have turned to Lincoln's life to clarify unresolved social conflicts that persist more than a century after his assassination.

Useful as it is to revisit such lives, it is equally valuable to explore those often neglected by biographers. Almost always, biographies are written about prominent individuals who changed, in some measure, the world around them. But who is prominent and what constitutes noteworthy change are matters of debate. Historical beauty is definitely in the eye of the beholder. That most American biographies tell of great white males and their untainted accomplishments speaks volumes about the society that produced such uncritical paeans. More recently, women and men of various racial, religious, and economic backgrounds have expanded the range of American biography. The lives of prominent African-American leaders, Native American chieftains, and immigrant sweatshop workers who climbed the success ladder to its top now crowd onto those library shelves next to familiar figures.

In the American Biographical History Series, specialists in key areas of American History describe the lives of important men and women of many different races, religions, and ethnic backgrounds as those figures shaped and were shaped by the political, social, economic, and cultural issues of their day and the people with whom they lived. Biographical subjects and readers share a dialogue across time and space as biographers pose the questions suggested by life in modern-day America to those who lived in other eras. Each life offers a timeless reservoir of answers to questions from the present. The result is at once edifying and entertaining.

The concise biographical portrait found in each volume in this series is enriched and made especially instructive by the attention paid to generational context. Each biographer has taken pains to link his or her subject to peers and predecessors engaged in the same area of accomplishment. Even the rare individuals whose ideas or behavior transcend their age operated within a broad social context of values, attitudes, and beliefs. Iconoclastic radicals, too, whatever their era, owed a debt to earlier generations of protesters and left a legacy for those who would resist the status quo in the future.

Biographers in the series offer readers new companions, individuals of accomplishment, whose lives and works can be weighed and assessed and consulted as resources in answering the nagging questions that the thoughtful in every generation ask of the past to better comprehend the present. The makers of America—male and female, black and white and red and yellow, Christian, Moslem, Jew, atheist, agnostic, and polytheist, rich and poor and in between—all testify with their lives that the past is prologue. Anxious to share his rich experiences with those willing to listen, an elderly Eastern European immigrant living in Pittsburgh boasted, "By myself, I'm a book!" He, too, realized that an important past could be explicated through the narrative of a life, in fact, his own.

When a biographer sees his or her subject in broader context, important themes are crystallized, an era is illuminated. The single life becomes a window to a past age and its truths for succeeding generations and for you.

ALAN M. KRAUT
JON L. WAKELYN

For Leslie

CONTENTS

The life of Fiorello H. La Guardia is fascinating, both because of his unique and colorful personal qualities as well as his position as a truly transitional figure who became a unifying bridge between generations of reformers and whole, widely disparate ethnic communities.

La Guardia the celebrity is best remembered by New Yorkers for his unusual antics—reading the comics over the radio, running into burning buildings, conducting the orchestra at park concerts. La Guardia the mayor is remembered as a tough taskmaster who provided an efficient, honest government that made numerous improvements to a city collapsing under the weight of Tammany corruption and the depression. This biographical essay analyzes La Guardia's tenure as mayor of New York, his relationships with such figures of his day as Jimmy Walker, Robert Moses, and Franklin Roosevelt, and his ability to forge a new federal-city partnership that still endures.

As the newer immigrant groups—Italians and Jews—forged their way into New York politics, La Guardia became symbolic leader of the ethnic political succession of his era. The mayor's relationship to the city's black community is also covered in detail. The conflicts and ethnic-based campaigns of the time, which pitted group against group, illustrate the ethnic tribalism endemic to America's multiethnic cities. Fiorello was motivated by ethnic and reform concerns and driven by enormous personal ambition. As U.S. congressman, mayor, leading progressive, New Deal advocate, and spokesman for Italian and Jewish aspirations and concerns, he filled many roles and had an impact far beyond the confines of New York.

Looking at La Guardia's life allows us to better understand the essence of the progressive movement, the impetus of urban reform, the impact of ethnicity and race on a major American city, the domestic repercussions of the rise of fascism in Europe, and the significance of New Deal largesse for cities. La Guardia was involved in so many of the major events of his time that a biography of him is akin to a history of the first half of the twentieth century. His role as a link between different eras will help readers understand the many complex problems and changes evident in America and provide needed background to comprehend the ethnic and political urban reform issues of present times.

This essay draws on my own primary research, but also builds upon the work of other historians who have written about La Guardia, his contemporaries, or his times. My debt then is not only to the libraries and archives that provided me with access to materials about La Guardia but to those who have worked these fields before me. Most particularly, Arthur Mann, Howard Zinn, and Thomas Kessner have influenced this study.

I would like to thank the series coeditors, Alan Kraut and Jon Wakelyn, for their useful critiques and encouragement. My thanks go also to the outside readers and Arthur Link, the publisher's general editor for history, for their helpful comments. Maureen Gilgore Hewitt, editor-in-chief of Harlan Davidson, also gave support at important moments. Most of all, my wife Leslie, as always, provided me with the moral support to complete what turned out to be an arduous task and shared her sharp insights for improving the manuscript. This book is dedicated to Leslie, with my love.

Ronald H. Bayor
Atlanta, Georgia

CHAPTER ONE

Bridging Different Worlds

The United States in the years from the end of the Civil War to the turn of the century was a country going through enormous changes. Industrialization spurred monopolization and concentration of wealth while providing Americans with cheaper and more plentiful products. Declining prices for farm products led farmers to form protest organizations to attempt to redress their grievances. In this age of materialism and greed, corporate influence in politics grew substantially. Union activity, some of it violent, intensified. The cities became overwhelmed by immigrants, particularly after 1882, when the source of immigration shifted from northern and western to southern and eastern Europe, and the numbers increased.

Many Americans became concerned about poverty in the midst of plenty, corrupt city governments, exploitation of workers, child labor, and the threat posed by the new industrial wealth to democratic institutions. As the nation tried to come to terms with industrialization and urbanization, responses varied. Some, such as financier J. P. Morgan, fit well into this period and reaped enormous profit from it. Others, such as Yale professor William Graham Sumner, became spokesmen for Social Darwinism, which justified the great wealth of the corporate entrepreneurs. Still others railed against the essence of the Gilded Age and offered criticisms and suggestions that would create a more equitable system and smooth away the harsh edges of nineteenth-century capitalism.

Fiorello Enrico (later Henry) La Guardia, born on December 11, 1882, in New York City in the midst of this turmoil, was to provide a unique response to the economic and social upheavals of his time. La Guardia bridged the era between the early years of protest against the industrial system and the later outburst of reform in the 1930s, and he took part in all the major issues and events of this period (immigration and ethnicity, progressivism, the fight against the urban political machines, World War I, the 1920s' conservative and nativistic reaction, the 1930s' economic collapse, Franklin Roosevelt's New Deal reforms, and World War II). He emerged as a spokesman for good-government forces, unions, immigrants, blacks, the urban poor, miners, and farmers. Fiorello connected the philosophies and activism of an earlier generation of reformers—among them, housing crusader Jacob Riis, Theodore Roosevelt, and Senators George Norris, Robert La Follette, and William Borah—to the later reformers of the New Deal generation. He interacted both with the older reform generation and with his own cohort in New York. The latter group provided various alternatives for coming to terms with the industrial age. James J. (Jimmy) Walker, born in 1881 and later mayor of New York, accepted and profited from the urban corruption of his times. Franklin D. Roosevelt, born in 1882, brought reform with new and surprising influence. Future governor and presidential candidate Alfred E. Smith, born in 1873; Robert F. Wagner, born in 1877 and a future United States senator; and Salvatore Cotillo, born in 1886 and later justice on the New York State Supreme Court, represented the Tammany political machine's approach to needed reform. (Tammany was New York County's Democratic party organization.)

The bridging of a generational gap among the reformers is only part of the La Guardia story. He also connected the values of the Old and New Worlds, immigrants and the native-born, and West and East. As such, La Guardia linked a New York City immigrant reform tradition represented by the socialist-oriented garment unions with the reform of middle America's farmer-labor groups. Moreover, as biographer Arthur Mann relates, La Guardia was "a marginal man who lived on the edge of many cultures." In addition to English, he could speak Yiddish, French, Italian, Hungarian, German, and Croatian. "Half-Jewish and half Italian, born in [New York's] Greenwich Village yet raised in Arizona, married first to a Catholic and then to a Lutheran but himself ... an Episcopalian, Fiorello La Guardia was a Mr. Brotherhood week all by himself." He was the product of many elements, all of which explain his personality, commitment, and accomplishments.

Family Background

When Fiorello was born in 1882 in an ethnically diverse section of Greenwich Village, large-scale Italian and eastern European Jewish migration to America was just beginning and would reach its peak in the early years of the twentieth century. His parents, Achille Luigi Carlo La Guardia and Irene Coen, had arrived in New York in 1880. What brought the La Guardias to the United States was Achille's music. His skill as a cornetist and arranger had led him in 1878 to tour the United States with Adelina Patti, a well-known Italian opera star. Achille, captivated by the New World, resolved during the tour that he would come back to live in America. After returning to Europe, he met and married Irene in 1880 in Trieste, Austria-Hungary, her birthplace, and then immigrated to the United States. Gemma, a daughter, was born in 1881, followed by Fiorello

(Little Flower) in 1882 and Richard in 1887. Had the La Guardias stayed in New York City, Fiorello would have grown up in a milieu of Irish political control through the Tammany machine and of competition among often contentious and striving ethnic groups over housing, jobs, political positions, and criminal operations. It was an environment that nurtured Jimmy Walker, Al Smith, and Robert Wagner, who moved easily up the political ladder, but that reluctantly offered only a few political positions to Italians. If America faced serious problems during a period of industrial growth and heavy immigration, New York City, where every problem seemed magnified, experienced wrenching times. Crime, poverty, ethnic conflict, corruption, labor violence, worker exploitation, disease, and inadequate housing were part of New York life. These problems were exacerbated by the depression of the 1890s.

To the Frontier

Fiorello would work to relieve these problems as New York's mayor and as a dominant force in New York's political world. However, in 1885, Achille, who had experienced difficulty finding steady work as a musician in New York, joined the army as chief musician in the Eleventh Infantry Regiment and moved his family west. It was a bold step for a newly arrived immigrant to leave the comfortable ethnic world of New York to venture to the western frontier. Achille, however, had traveled extensively before his marriage, and wanted his family to identify themselves as Americans rather than as Italian immigrants. Fiorello was thereby provided with a unique childhood and a different perspective from the one he would have learned in the overcrowded tenements of New York. The La Guardias moved a number of times—from Fort Sully in North Dakota to Madison Barracks, Sackett's Harbor, New York to Fort Huachuca, Arizona Territory, and finally, in 1892, to

Whipple Barracks near Prescott, Arizona Territory. By this time Achille had become a bandmaster. The small western frontier town of Prescott, rather than New York's multiethnic neighborhoods, became La Guardia's childhood home.

The West of the 1880s and 1890s still had elements of frontier life, although they were fast disappearing. Nonetheless, soldiers, cowboys, miners, Indians, gamblers, and outlaws inhabited Fiorello's world. The Indian Wars were in their last years but Arizona Territory contained a number of tribes—Apaches, Hopi, Pima, and Navajos. This was the sparsely settled frontier into which both American civilization and culture were expanding and by which they were being shaped, as historian Frederick Jackson Turner noted in 1893. It was a vast area that helped form the American characteristics of individualism, nationalism, and democracy. It was also a West of railroad-labor conflicts, and corrupt government Indian agents. All of these aspects of Western life were to influence the young Fiorello.

In his autobiography, Fiorello pointed to some particular events in Arizona that, he asserted, shaped his personality, thinking, and subsequent life. For example, La Guardia observed how the Indian agents, all politically appointed, cheated the Indians. "This was," La Guardia stated, "my first contact with 'politicians.'" Fiorello noted that his hatred for professional politicians and political machines began while he was still a child. Along with the agents in Fiorello's demonology were professional gamblers, or "tinhorns," an epithet he would frequently hurl at New York's corrupt public officials and gangsters. These early observations coalesced for the impressionable young La Guardia when he later began reading the Sunday edition of Joseph Pulitzer's *New York World*, which the family received in Prescott. This newspaper's incessant attacks on New York's Tammany machine and its revelations of corruption in that city during the 1890s, particularly in the police department, gave more focus to Fiorello's anger at political corruption. "A resentment against Tammany was created in me at that time," he later said, "which I admit is to this day almost an obsession." Coupled with a general resentment of authority figures, evident early in his life, La Guardia's later challenge to the established politicians was almost predictable.

Reform Beginnings

The historical and national context for La Guardia's early animosity towards corruption and Tammany was the beginning stages of the Progressive movement in the 1890s. Responding to the myriad social, political, and economic problems Americans faced at that time, various reformers emerged to offer solutions. For example, in the 1890s and early years of the twentieth century, reform mayors were elected in a number of cities to challenge the corrupt politicians and greedy utility and transportation company officials who through franchise deals and high prices were robbing the public. In some cases, such as in Toledo with Samuel ("Golden Rule") Jones (elected in 1897) or a few years later in Cleveland with Tom Johnson (1901), dynamic and honest mayors dealt with corruption, made government more efficient, and provided a better existence for the inhabitants of their cities.

Progressivism in the early twentieth century built on the protests of the Populists (the rural-based reform movement of the 1890s), the good-government supporters, the believers in the social gospel (a clerical-based advocacy for social reform), the muckraking journalists (writers who exposed avarice and corruption in American life), and the effort to provide a better environment for the poor and a more orderly, conflict-free one for business. From these elements, Progressivism emerged with a thrust toward more democracy, an increase in government power and efficiency in order to solve the many economic and social problems of the country which had been exacerbated by the 1890s depression, and a moral imperative to deal with the abuses of industrial society.

This dominating reform movement of the period attracted many individuals from various backgrounds. Businessmen, clergy, journalists, and even Tammany machine politicians such as Al Smith and Robert Wagner were drawn to the movement. It also was to attract the anti-Tammany La Guardia, but not until later. In the early stages of his political career, Fiorello's progressive philosophy was still forming, but even then his interests and concerns were the same as many of the progressives. In 1937, La Guardia, then mayor of New York City, commented on how much he had been influenced by reading Jacob Riis's *How the Other Half Lives* in 1903. With his strong resentment of corruption and special privilege, and his moral outrage when "they" (the powerful, corrupt, greedy elements of society) cheated the poor, Fiorello was at heart a progressive long before his thinking about reform fully matured.

In addition to the plight of the Indians, La Guardia was affected by how poorly workers were treated in the late nineteenth century, a period of intense labor-management friction. During this time workers who were trying to organize to achieve higher wages and shorter hours often encountered an implacable management that was able to call on a sympathetic federal government for the means to break strikes. Child labor was extensive, and workers endured low wages, long hours, and little compensation if they were injured on the job. The railroad industry was among the most abusive in the nation. As with many newly settled areas of the West, Prescott saw extensive railroad construction as the western lines were expanded. La Guardia, a sensitive boy attuned to the sufferings of others, was struck by how poorly the rail workers were treated as they constructed the line near Prescott. He saw very quickly that the workers, who often were immigrants, were regarded as machines, not people, by the bosses. "If a laborer was injured he lost his job," noted La Guardia. "Even as a young boy, this struck me as all wrong, and I thought about it a great deal." According to this future spokesman for workers' rights, the Prescott experience developed his awareness of the need to protect workers. "It was this early glimpse of the condition of working people, of their exploitation and their utter lack of protection under the law, which prompted me to take an interest on their side in society."

In 1894, the Pullman strike shut down the nation's railroads and culminated in a violent outburst. Railroad workers in Eugene Debs's American Railway Union fought for their rights as workers and clashed first with the Pullman Company, and then with a coalition of railroad company executives called the General Managers' Association. Finally, when efforts to get the men back to work under a court injunction failed, the army was brought in against the workers. La Guardia, who was twelve at the time, saw soldiers being used to protect railroad property and to keep laborers from congregating and airing their grievances. He later recalled that he thought at the time that the workers were being treated unjustly and that labor problems could be dealt with in a way that was fair to both workers and management.

Early on, then, La Guardia showed a budding progressivism, a concern with workers and strikes, and a western sense of individuality and open spaces. He was therefore in perfect tune with the emerging western, and often Republican, progressives such as La Follette and Norris, whom La Guardia would support later on. As New Deal advisor and La Guardia aide Rexford Tugwell noted:

It must never be forgotten that La Guardia was actually a West-erner, and typically western in his intentions and reactions. . . . His was a breed familiar to American politics. Among his con-temporaries—some actually older, some younger than he, but active at the same time—were [Senator Burton K.] Wheeler [Montana], [Senator] Norris [Nebraska], the two La Follettes [the sons of Robert La Follette: Philip and Robert, Jr., of Wis-consin], [Governor] Floyd Olson [Minnesota], and numerous associates in the House, such as Tom Amlie [Wisconsin]; and these were the people with which he felt a close kinship, with whom he liked to be, and whose motives he understood and approved.

Fiorello viewed himself as a westerner even during his years in New York where he could easily be spotted wearing his western-style hat.

An Outsider

However, one factor made him remain very much an outsider and gave him a different perspective from the western progressives. Fiorello's father was an Italian immi-grant and his mother, although born in Trieste, Austria-Hungary, came out of an Italian-Jewish background. Fior-ello's identification with the hordes of southern and eastern Europeans streaming into the country in the 1890s con-nected him forever with these new groups just as if he had been reared in New York's crowded immigrant districts. Achille wanted his children to identify with what he viewed as "American." They attended a Protestant Sunday school in Prescott, were raised as Episcopalians, and spoke En-glish at home. However, to his peers in Prescott, La Guar-dia was an Italian (his maternal Jewish ancestry not yet being publicly known or emphasized).

One incident reveals how Fiorello was affected by this identification. When he was about ten, an organ-grinder with a monkey came to Prescott. The children gathered around to watch, and they soon began to taunt La Guardia.

They called out, "A dago with a monkey! Hey Fiorello, you're a dago too. Where's your monkey?" La Guardia was mortified, and more so when his father, speaking Italian, asked the organ-grinder to their house for dinner. Fiorello was teased cruelly by the other children because of this incident. The long-term impact was evident after La Guardia had become mayor. He forbade organ-grinders to use New York's streets, an action difficult to explain without knowledge of his embarrassment in Prescott. Nonetheless, the more significant factor is that regardless of his father's efforts, Fiorello was clearly made aware that he was a "marginal man," on the outside of the American culture. At one point he called himself Frank in order to sound more American, but then reverted to his original name. And years later, when his thoughts turned to seeking the presidency, he often said that his name limited his chances to move up in politics. His sense of "marginality" remained a part of his makeup.

La Guardia was defensive about his ancestry and became a fervent supporter of the immigrant populations and a fighter for the respect due them. As he noted in his autobiography: "It always annoys me greatly whenever I hear thoughtless people, often raised the easy way, who have never known any of the hardships these immigrant families endured every day, hurl insults at American citizens who have in many cases contributed more to the welfare of this nation than those who look down upon them or turn their noses up to them."

Rage and Resentment

La Guardia combined his sensitivity about his ethnicity and his concern for the have-nots with a belligerency that some have attributed to his small stature. As an adult, Fiorello was a little over five feet tall and had a slight build. His sister claimed that Fiorello tried to stand out in other ways—by being aggressive and talkative—and was very self-conscious about his height. In one youthful incident, Fiorello was fighting a taller boy and his fists could not get near the boy's face. Rather than give up, La Guardia found a chair, jumped on top of it, and started fighting again. He never gave up. Later on, when he was mayor and an aide made a remark about a job seeker being too short, La Guardia flew into a rage and shouted, "What's the matter with a little guy? What's the matter with a little guy? What's the matter with a little guy?" And this was from a man who always kept a bust of Napoleon on his desk.

His belligerence was directed at all around him, even those he loved and respected. Fiorello at times would curse at his father, and when one of his teachers graded some incorrect math answers as right, Fiorello showed her the mistakes and said, "Look here, teacher, you better learn arithmetic if you are going to teach us." Achille had difficulty controlling his son. Like his father, Fiorello was independent-minded, mischievous, rash, and stubborn.

Rage and resentment and (also like his father) a toughness combined with sensitivity and concern made up Fiorello's character. He loved music, and had a gentle side, but was also as tough as any street-corner politician. As a child, he learned to play the banjo and cornet from his overly critical father, who screamed at him when he made a mistake. Fiorello would respond by saying, "Keep on screaming Papa, in this way I'll learn." Yet he was also later to be touchy about criticism, mistrustful of others, and resentful toward authority. Like his father, he was a very demanding overseer who was unlikely to praise his subordinates, although he was likely to worry about their welfare. The future mayor borrowed his leadership style from his father. The imperious maestro led his band as Fiorello would later lead the city—with a strong hand. Fiorello loved the leadership role, even as a young boy, and enjoyed being the center of attention. With his short stature and high voice, however, La Guardia did not seem to be someone who would be able to take on the often vicious Tammany and bring New Yorkers into a period of reform.

The Impact of War

La Guardia graduated from grammar school in January 1898. He began the ninth grade but never finished because of the outbreak of the Spanish-American War in April 1898. This war was to change Fiorello's life and add yet another resentment against "them," "the interests" (the powerful, corrupt, greedy elements of society), a resentment which he would carry with him the rest of his life. Fiorello's father, along with the Eleventh Infantry, was transferred to Jefferson Barracks, near St. Louis, in April 1898, then to Mobile, Alabama, and eventually to Cuba. The families stayed at Jefferson Barracks. Fiorello at first tried to enlist, but his age and size kept him out of the army. Determined to follow his father to Mobile and then to Cuba, Fiorello secured a job at age fifteen as a war correspondent with the *St. Louis Post-Dispatch*. When the Eleventh Infantry moved on to Tampa, Florida, en route to Cuba, Fiorello went too, but there the war ended for him and his father. Achille became sick, as did so many other soldiers during this war, from rotten meat sold to the army. The federal government would eventually take action against the abusive meat-packing companies when Theodore Roosevelt assumed the presidency, but for now many suffered from an industry that cared little that consumers were fed tainted meat. Upton Sinclair's muckraking novel, *The Jungle*, was to expose the problems of this industry in 1906.

Achille never fully recovered. He was sent back to Jefferson Barracks, and soon after was honorably discharged from the army because of his medical problems. Fiorello went to St. Louis with his father, and after a brief stay in New York in 1898, the family sailed back to Europe, giving up on the New World experience. Hoping to make a new start in Trieste, Achille entered into business. Although he ultimately did well with a hotel he leased, he did not live long enough to enjoy his success. In 1904, at fifty-five, Achille died from heart problems. Fiorello was convinced that the rotten meat of army days had destroyed his father's health. He was also angry that his mother was denied a pension based on her claim that Achille's death was service-related. As a congressman, Fiorello, in one of the first acts of his political career, proposed a bill that required the death penalty for those who sold inferior or tainted supplies to the army in wartime and a long jail term in peacetime. Fiorello had been affected personally by the abuse and greed of the industrial age—no longer just an observer of corrupt Indian agents and unfair railroad companies, Fiorello was now a victim. His father was dead after an aborted career and his family was plunged into poverty. This incident was the final boyhood lesson and explains at least in part his attraction to reform later on.

The Consular Years

In need of money, Fiorello secured a job in 1900 as a clerk at the American consulate in Budapest. In 1903 he moved on to Fiume, a Hungarian port, to serve as the acting and then permanent consular agent. It was in these positions that La Guardia showed his intelligence, ability to learn quickly, and independence. He mastered several languages—German, Croatian, French, Hungarian, Italian, and Yiddish—and therefore could understand the languages of many of the immigrants going to America. La Guardia also saw the immigrants' suffering and became their champion. Ambitious, status-hungry, enjoying the power of the consular agent's position, and touched by the plight of the migrating Balkan population, La Guardia turned this relatively low-level job into a stepping-stone and educational experience for himself. He also became a gadfly to his superiors.

Two incidents reflect La Guardia's concerns and independence. He became aware as consular agent in Fiume that the procedure for medical inspection of immigrants was faulty. Prospective immigrants would sail to America, and upon arriving at Ellis Island in New York harbor face a complete medical exam that might discover a condition that made them ineligible for entry. Families then had to face an arduous return journey to Europe with their funds exhausted or, worse, had to decide to enter America without one or more family members who had to return to the Old World. Financial ruin or family separation—neither was a good choice for people already going through difficult times. La Guardia came up with a solution that should have been obvious to any immigration official. Rather than a very superficial attempt at judging the immigrants' health before sailing, which had been the practice of consuls, he began providing potential immigrants with full medical examinations before they left Fiume. He refused to allow the ships to sail unless this was done and thereby delayed the departure times and angered officials of the steamship line. Nonetheless, under La Guardia's procedure fewer immigrants were refused entry when they arrived in America from Fiume than from other ports. Many years later this procedure was made official policy for all immigrants leaving for America.

On another occasion, Fiorello received a request for the immediate embarkation of immigrants so that Maria Josefa, archduchess of Austria, could watch the immigrants board. This meant keeping the immigrants below decks for three days until the scheduled sailing time. La Guardia, only twenty-two at the time, refused to accede to the archduchess's wishes because of his concern for the immigrants. After complaints from the royal family, La Guardia was transferred to Trieste. Standing up to these officials was a prelude to his standing up to powerful politicians and bureaucrats in the United States and battling for people's rights. He was fiercely independent, unwilling to back down to authority, especially when he felt his cause was just, and deeply concerned about the downtrodden in society. In addition, however, he enjoyed the attention his antics brought.

Because he had antagonized influential people in the Austro-Hungarian government and caused problems for the U.S. State Department, La Guardia did not get promoted. He was still ambitious, however, and wanted to make a name for himself in America. Fiorello therefore resigned in 1906 from the consular service and returned to New York, leaving his mother, sister, and brother behind in Budapest.

"The test is if you hesitate."

Fiorello arrived in a city that was undergoing vast changes as it absorbed the great waves of humanity flowing in from abroad. From the Lower East Side of Manhattan (where thousands of newly arrived Jews and Italians settled) to Harlem and on to the boroughs of the Bronx and Brooklyn (which caught the overflow of this migration as well as earlier immigrants who were moving to better housing), New York seemed at times to be bursting at the seams. New York was the entire world in microcosm. The sounds and scents of Warsaw, Palermo, Dublin, Bucharest, Berlin, and Canton filled the streets, and such labels as Little Italy, Kleindeutschland, the Jewish ghetto, and Chinatown were applied to the city's neighborhoods. In the immigrant quarters, pushcart vendors selling fruits and vegetables, small shops with their wares spilling out onto the sidewalk, crowded tenements with cluttered fire escapes, and open fire hydrants cooling off the neighborhood children during the summer were part of the usual street scenes. New York was noisy, crowded, gritty, poor, and filled with immigrants, but it also had quiet, secluded, wealthy residential areas where old-stock Americans lived in magnificent homes.

Fiorello worked at a variety of jobs in New York before settling into a position in November 1907 as an interpreter at Ellis Island. He also served briefly in 1910 as an interpreter at night court. La Guardia again became aware of human suffering, for during these peak years of migration to America, Ellis Island was packed daily with thousands of frightened and confused immigrants from many lands. The immigrants' lives opened up to La Guardia as he interpreted the rules for them, saw where they went to live in the city, and helped them deal with various bureaucratic problems. He not only saw their plight at close range but he also saw Tammany's abuse and corruption, the graft in the police department and among city officials that he had only read about before. When the young La Guardia was assigned to night court, an immigration inspector issued the following warning: "You can get experience in this job, or you can make a great deal of money. I don't think you'll take the money. But, remember, the test is if you hesitate. Unless you say 'No!' right off, the first time an offer comes your way, you're gone." Fiorello never hesitated.

The Power of Tammany

Tammany was in its heyday during these years and followed the dictates of its 1890s boss, Richard Croker, who stated that "he was in politics for what he could get out of it." The rising tide of immigrants and the burgeoning power of the political machine worked hand in hand. Tammany provided the newly arrived with jobs, social welfare, and, at times, political recognition in return for votes. Corruption, payoffs, and patronage were the machine's lifeblood. Although it often claimed to be the protector of the immigrants, Tammany clearly worked against them in numerous ways, such as by taking bribes to neglect housing regulations. Although reform mayoral administrations occasionally won by running on fusion (joint or merged) tickets (e.g., Seth Low in 1901 and John Purroy Mitchel in 1913) and investigations such as that of the Lexow Committee in the 1890s revealed Tammany corruption, the machine always rebounded back into power. It even extended its control, dominating all the borough Democratic organizations by 1909. By using the police and criminals and at times by making deals with Republicans to stay in power, Tammany remained a formidable force in New York City politics.

The machine became even stronger under boss Charles F. Murphy's reign (1902–1924). Murphy had the foresight to develop capable young politicians such as Al Smith, Robert Wagner, and Salvatore Cotillo within Tammany and at times to support progressive measures. Smith, for example, a product of New York's Irish slums, rose quickly in Tammany ranks. He was at first just a political hack, but he grew and changed while a state assemblyman, particularly after delving into the causes of the terrible Triangle Shirtwaist Company fire in 1911, which claimed numerous lives. As vice-chairman of the New York State Factory Investigating Commission, which functioned from 1911 to 1914, Smith came to understand the abusive labor conditions that were evident in industrial America and that were a factor in the many deaths in the Triangle disaster. During and after his work on the commission, Smith became a strong advocate of reform and helped to convince Tammany that some legislation was needed to help the working class. Wagner followed the same course. Growing up poor (his father was a janitor), the son of German immigrants, Wagner saw the Tammany machine as the key to success. He rose fast in Democratic politics and was elected to the state assembly and senate (and later to the U.S. Senate). Although his reform impulse blossomed earlier than Smith's, it was not until the Triangle fire and his work as chairman of the investigating commission that he too became a major supporter of social welfare legislation. Cotillo, raised in East Harlem's Little Italy, entered politics as an opponent of Tammany. Following entreaties from Tammany, Cotillo joined the machine in 1912. He believed that only through Tammany could he help his people. Moving up in its ranks, although more slowly and with more opposition than Smith and Wagner, Cotillo emerged as an important advocate of social reform. Murphy, according to Smith, was concerned about social legislation too, but other evidence indicates that he also saw his backing of reform issues as a way of winning votes and appeasing the reformers in the party. He was agreeable to change as long as it did not hurt the machine. As historian David Burner comments, "If Murphy gave his blessing to some reforms, he stood in the way of many more." And he expected his subordinates to follow his lead, and that indicated the limitations of a boss-run government. If it was not outright corrupt, it was curtailed in its vision. Murphy, although he did eliminate some corrupt practices, still thought of the survival of the machine above all else. After he died in 1924, corruption and graft became rampant again.

A People's Attorney

The New York of Tammany, immigrants, reform-fusion mayors, corruption, and progressivism was La Guardia's world after his return in 1906. Always ambitious, and forever interested in improving himself, Fiorello enrolled in New York University's evening law school in 1907 after securing his high school diploma and passing the qualifying examinations. La Guardia worked during the day at Ellis Island and rushed to school at night (except in the last year of law school, when he worked at night court and went to school in the day). These were busy years in which La

Guardia demonstrated what was to be a lifetime capacity for hard work and long hours. Fiorello was graduated from law school (with mediocre grades) in 1910, passed the bar, quit the job at Ellis Island, and began a career as a lawyer. He rented space in an established law firm's office and began to specialize in immigrant issues, such as deportation cases. His concern for the immigrant poor and his willingness to provide legal advice free of charge or at low rates earned him a reputation as a "people's attorney" in the Lower East Side area where he worked. In 1912 Fiorello and Raimondo Canudo (a lawyer and editor of a newspaper for Sicilians) set up their own law office and focused their practice on immigrant problems.

As was true of his Ellis Island years, his law practice was an educational experience for La Guardia. His western boyhood and middle-class background had distanced him from the experiences of Italian peasant immigrants. He now was pulled into their world as well as that of their Jewish neighbors on the Lower East Side. His ability to speak Italian and Yiddish enabled La Guardia to do legal work for the immigrant population, which he continued to do when he became a partner in the firm of Weil, La Guardia and Espen in 1914. It was at this time that he gained first-hand knowledge of New York's court system and its unfair and corrupt practices, arbitrary decisions, and politically influenced judgments, all of which inspired his move into politics to correct the system and served him well later as a reformer of the courts. He also saw the need to improve government so as to provide equitable treatment for the average citizen. It was during this period as well that he met Marie Fischer, later to be his second wife, who worked as his secretary.

Fiorello's law work drew him into union activities at a time when unions were still fighting for recognition and workers endured long hours, low pay, and mistreatment in sweatshops. During a garment workers' strike in 1912, he gladly offered his services to the union after his friend August Bellanca, one of the strike leaders, asked for his help. Given his earlier reaction in Prescott to the Pullman strike and his knowledge of the problems of the poverty-stricken immigrants, it is not surprising that La Guardia championed the union cause. His later views that workers had a right to strike, that government should protect that right, and that there should be a process for avoiding strikes were forged by the Prescott and New York experiences. The union asked La Guardia to help bring together Jewish and Italian workers in the common cause. Fiorello was effective with the ethnic groups and also was active at the union hall, on the picket line, and in the courts.

The strike was a turning point for the future mayor. He developed ties with union officials; made his first speech; met various socialist leaders, such as Meyer London (later a congressman) and labor lawyer Jacob Panken, whom he would sometimes support and sometimes conflict with in years to come; established himself as a labor lawyer; and became an active participant in New York's growing union movement in the garment trades. He also met Thea Almerigotti, an Italian immigrant from Trieste, who worked as a dress designer and who became his first wife. The workers so appreciated Fiorello's talents and efforts that he became part of a three-member committee assigned to work out a final agreement with management. From this point on La Guardia's connections with the unions were strong. For example, he continued into the 1920s as a volunteer lawyer for District Council 1's Italian section. The council was made up of affiliates of the United Garment Workers. La Guardia also made his initial contact with the beginning Amalgamated Clothing Workers Union of America, which emerged as a result of this strike. This was the first of many labor conflicts in which La Guardia would offer his talents to settle the dispute peacefully.

Not Politics as Usual

As an ambitious lawyer and union activist who was in touch with and concerned about the immigrant ghetto populations and disgusted by corruption in the courts and politics, Fiorello was well placed for a try at running for political office. But it was not going to be politics as usual for Fiorello. Although he wanted power and respect, he also was scrupulously honest and independent, and was outraged by the powerful interests, crooks, and grafting politicians who oppressed and cheated the people. As he stated, "I had been storing up knowledge, and I was eager to bring about better conditions, particularly a more equitable economic situation and less favoritism to special interests in the administration of the law." An incipient progressive, a people's attorney motivated by ethnic and reform factors, La Guardia began a political career that would bring him fame as a dynamic reformer and as a vocal spokesman for the new immigrants and the poor.

CHAPTER TWO

A Fighting Congressman

La Guardia in 1906 decided to join the Republican party in New York, which once again made him an outsider in the Democrat-controlled city. But, as he noted, "I joined the Republican Party because I could not stomach . . . the Democratic political machine." It was a logical step for Fiorello, and one that many outsiders—primarily Italians and Jews—in New York's Irish-run city could understand. Not all agreed with 1920s Tammany boss George Olvany's statement that "the Irish are natural leaders. The strain of Limerick keeps them at the top. They have the ability to handle men. Even the Jewish districts have Irish leaders. The Jews want to be ruled by them." Although German-Americans such as Robert F. Wagner had received Tammany's support, and some concessions had been given to the newly arrived southern and eastern European immigrant groups, the Irish remained in firm control.

Ethnic Realities

Jews as a group, because of defections to the other parties and growing political strength, had been given more recognition in New York politics than Italians, but neither group had as many political positions as it desired. The

Italians, poorly organized politically, having many non-citizens within their group, suffered with little political power for a long time. They also were more inclined than Jews to vote for the Tammany ticket. Therefore, the Democrats concentrated on winning Jewish support. However, Tammany did provide some positions for Italians. For example, Salvatore Cotillo was elected in 1912 to the New York State Assembly. He later went to the state senate and in 1923 became the first Italian justice on the New York Supreme Court. But the politicians who controlled his nominations for office were Irish. The reluctance to bring an ethnic newcomer along too quickly and to share power with new groups was evident. Another example was Michael Rofrano, who, as an aide to Tom Foley, a powerful Tammany leader, worked to bring Italians into the Democratic fold. However, when in 1912 Rofrano desired to be repaid for his efforts with a congressional nomination, he was turned down and even laughed at by Foley, who was not willing to put an Italian in as congressman.

La Guardia's generation of New York Italians therefore faced slow going in the Democratic party. Even into the 1930s, when Italians were given important political positions, it was usually in areas where the Republicans were making a major bid for the Italian vote and where the ethnic group's displeasure had to be addressed. The lack of attention to Italians was described by Alfred Santangelo, an Italian political leader and a congressman during the 1950s and 1960s:

> Staten Island, where I grew up, was dominated by the Irish. The Congressman, the Senator and one or two Assemblymen were Irish. The other Assemblyman and the City Councilman were of German extraction. All the judges were Irish. No judge was of Italian descent. No Italian-American was considered for public office, although the Italian-Americans constituted about 25 percent of the Staten Island population.

"A Stepping-Stone for . . . Other Italians"

Given La Guardia's already evident anti-Tammany feelings, the Democratic party's frequent neglect of the Italian
vote, and his unwillingness to embrace socialism, it was predictable that the ambitious Fiorello would find a home in
the Republican party and organize the Italian community
from that base. He was not the only young, ambitious Italian American who joined the Republicans. Another notable example is Edward Corsi who created the Italian
Republican League in 1925 and the Columbian Republican
League of the State of New York in 1926. Corsi's work for
the Republicans bore fruit when he was named state commissioner of immigration and naturalization in 1931 and
became the Republican candidate for the U.S. Senate in
1938 (the first Italian American to run for this position).
Fiorello found many other young, ambitious Italians who
shared both his desire to achieve political recognition for
their group and his distaste for Tammany.

The group La Guardia joined in 1906 was the Twenty-
fifth Assembly District Republican Club, located in a section of lower Manhattan populated by Irish, Italians, and
old-stock Americans. Here he learned his first lessons in
practical politics and slowly climbed in the organization,
becoming an election district captain in 1912. Aided by individuals such as Louis Espresso, Mike Kehoe, and Harry
G. Andrews, all professional politicians as sharp as any in
Tammany, La Guardia learned quickly. Espresso, a fellow
Italian, stated years later, "I personally was interested [in
La Guardia] because I figured that with a man like La
Guardia I was making a stepping-stone for the other Italians in this great city. . . . I wanted to do something for my
forefathers that came to this country, . . . that their sons
and daughters etc. would get a better chance in politics because in those days the Italians were a nonentity." Although
still imbued with his negative attitude toward professional

politicians, La Guardia accepted the advice of these individuals, mastered the trade, and got to know the district.
During this early period, he stayed a regular Republican—
even in 1912 when Theodore Roosevelt broke with the
party to lead a short-lived reformist Progressive party and
in 1913 when some Republicans supported the reform fusion mayoral candidate, John Purroy Mitchel.

La Guardia became acquainted with the leadership of
the Italian community in the district. Helped by a group of
his friends, also young Italian-Americans, Fiorello began to
create his ethnic organizational base. Antonio Calitri, a
poet, and Giovanni Fabrizio, a musician, introduced La
Guardia to the leaders of various Italian associations.
August Bellanca, as already noted, brought Fiorello into
union activities. La Guardia felt close to these friends, who
shared his ethnic background, cultural interests, and social
class. They supported La Guardia's political ambitions in
these early years, hoping, like Espresso, that he would lead
the Italian community out of their political and economic
powerlessness.

Fiorello had indicated his interest in political office as
early as 1911, when he tried and failed to secure an appointment as deputy state attorney general. In 1914 he saw
another opportunity for advancement. The Fourteenth
Congressional District, which contained the Twenty-fifth
Assembly District and was a Tammany stronghold, was in
need of a Republican candidate. The individual chosen initially had decided not to run. This district had never
elected a Republican congressman and there were not
many who wanted to run in a "hopeless" contest. La Guardia, however, was ambitious and confident that he could
make a good race. He therefore offered himself as a candidate when the Republican bosses meeting in his political
clubhouse asked if anyone there wanted to run for this office. La Guardia was accepted, although he almost lost the
nomination when the person putting the candidates'

names on nominating petitions wanted someone whose name was easier to spell.

His Democratic opponent, Michael Farley, assumed a victory and did not even campaign. Fiorello, however, hit the ground running. He had a number of useful skills that would make this race closer than expected including his fluency in Italian and Yiddish. He kept up a barrage of attacks on Tammany wherever he could find a crowd or create one. Going from door to door, speaking on street corners and attending numerous weddings and other events, Fiorello fought hard for victory. He emphasized his European experience and his union work in his appeals to the immigrant, working-class people of the area. Although the Republican party had no hope of Fiorello winning and gave him no campaign money, he was able to canvass the district with the help of his Italian friends and put on a credible campaign.

As expected, La Guardia lost, by only about 1,700 votes, but did better than any previous Republican and substantially reduced the size of the Democratic vote. The campaign honed Fiorello's political style and defined his issues. He emerged as a hard-hitting, tireless campaigner who was vehemently anti-Tammany and deeply concerned with the needs of immigrants, workers, and the poor in general. The Republican bosses now saw La Guardia as someone with a political future who could reach out to the immigrant masses.

"What Are You in Politics for, for Love?"

As a reward for his good showing and hard work for the party, Fiorello was made deputy attorney general of New York State. This was not an important appointment and was designed simply to provide a good candidate with a job. Fiorello wanted a different position, that of appraiser, which paid more. However, no post was unimportant to him, and even this minor position could be used to further his career, fight the interests, and defend the underprivileged. He began proceedings against New Jersey factories that polluted the air in Manhattan. This case had dragged on for years with no compliance by the companies. La Guardia moved aggressively against the interstate polluters and sought to bring the issue before the U.S. Supreme Court. As in his earlier consular days, La Guardia was not afraid to take on the powerful. Nonetheless, also as earlier, his actions brought a rebuke from his superiors, who wanted Fiorello to spend his time preparing the case but not actually trying to get the companies to comply. These companies had friends in high state office and nothing had been done against them over the years because of this protection. As La Guardia commented later, "The party big shots were closely connected with the matter. These corporations had used their tremendous influence, and I was given orders to take no action from now on unless I got direct approval [from those in higher office]."

He learned the same lesson again—that the wealthy and powerful were politically protected—when he tried to take action against some large oyster companies on Long Island for violating the state's conservation law regarding the catching of scallops. In this situation, the case was delayed long enough for the state legislature to rewrite the law in order to exempt the bigger companies from its provisions. In a final case, La Guardia sought legal redress against large meat-packing companies that were violating the weights and measures law. Again political favoritism prevented him from making the companies comply. The political protectionism that was evident in all three cases involved not just the hated Tammany, which was to be expected, but also the state Republican leadership which served to increase La Guardia's animosity towards professional politicians. In the last situation, Fiorello also received a political lesson from future mayor Jimmy

Walker, then a state senator and a rising star in Tammany ranks. Walker, who had written the weights and measures law, now defended the meat-packing companies who were violating it and won the case in New York City's magistrates' court. As Fiorello describes the situation in his autobiography, he asked Walker how he could take a case in which he would work against his own law. Walker replied, "Fiorello, when are you going to get wise? Why do you suppose we introduce bills? We introduce them sometimes just to kill them. Other times we even have to pass a bill. Why are you in the Attorney General's office? You're not going to stay there all your life. You make your connections now, and later on you can pick up a lot of dough defending cases you are now prosecuting." The judge agreed with Walker's appraisal. La Guardia, however, was concerned that although the big companies had been protected and cleared, small shopkeepers were still being fined for the same offense. Walker advised La Guardia to "stop worrying about those things. What are you in politics for, for love?" This experience left Fiorello disgusted with both parties, but politically wiser than before.

"We Didn't Double-Cross You"
The 1916 Campaign

Even as deputy attorney general, La Guardia's eyes were on the congressional seat he had campaigned for in 1914. In a sense the campaign had never stopped. Getting the nomination in 1916 took some work, however. The Republicans were ready to choose another candidate, who could secure big contributions for the party. Fiorello was told to "just be a good boy, go along with the organization, help whenever you can." La Guardia refused to accept that advice. Instead, he boldly threatened to run against the party's choice in the Republican primaries. His aggressive ambition coupled with state chairman Fred Tanner's belated decision to back Fiorello if he wanted to run for this office so strongly, secured the nomination. He also captured the Progressive party nomination, his first official tie to the progressive label. Once again the Democratic opponent was Farley.

A smart campaign and tactics that he would use many times in the future made La Guardia a formidable campaigner. He realized early on that he would be fighting not only Tammany but also his own Republican district leaders. (New York Republicans often cooperated with the powerful Democrats in return for favors.) Election cheating was very easy at that time because the paper ballots then in use could easily be altered. A ballot counter could do this by hiding a piece of pencil lead under his fingernail and making extra marks on the ballot, thereby invalidating it, or, alternatively, by simply substituting a new ballot with the "correct" vote for one taken out of the pack with the "wrong" vote. La Guardia prepared for such dirty tricks by gathering a group of volunteers, including some who were good at fighting, to oversee the ballot count and keep the vote honest. It was not always the people's choice who won, and Tammany was well versed in how to fix elections.

La Guardia's campaign centered on an effective strategy. In a poor, immigrant area during World War I, ethnic and worker issues were sure to have an appeal. Fiorello was good at exploiting both. As he noted, "In my talks on the East Side I dismembered the Hapsburg Empire and liberated all the subjugated countries under that dynasty almost every night." Using ethnicity as a vote-getting tactic was hardly unknown and had long been in Tammany's bag of tricks. But La Guardia was especially good at wooing the ethnic voter. Robert Moses, La Guardia's parks commissioner in his mayoral years, later commented that "in exploiting racial and religious prejudices La Guardia could run circles around the bosses he despised and derided. When it came to raking ashes of Old World hates, warming ancient grudges, waving the bloody shirt, tuning the ear to ancestral voices, he could easily outdemagogue the demagogues." In 1916 this was easy to do: by appealing to Germans, Italians, Jews, Irish, and others, he picked up the support of various ethnic leaders and newspapers, including the traditionally Democratic German-language *New Yorker Staats-Zeitung*. Farley was outsmarted, especially because he represented the party of President Woodrow Wilson. Wilson was castigated for his pro-British "neutrality" and his accusations that the foreign-born supported their ancestral homelands instead of adhering to America's neutral position.

La Guardia won the election by 357 votes out of over 18,000. It was a close election, but Tammany had been defeated in one of its strongholds. The following anecdote illustrates what La Guardia was up against in this district. When he returned to his Republican clubhouse after the victory, he heard one of the politicians talking on the telephone in the back room to the Democratic leader of the district and apologizing, saying, "No, Joe, we didn't doublecross you; we didn't do anything for this fellow. You just can't control him." That was politics in New York and, as La Guardia says in his autobiography, "Those are just some of the little things that have made me an incurable insurgent." La Guardia's tactics and precautions had worked, and this fervent, emotional, hard-hitting, and sometimes demagogic campaigner would use them again in numerous campaigns.

Protecting America's Rights

The election put La Guardia into a position where he could do some good and achieve the respect and status he craved. But as one among many representatives, how much could he really do and would the congressional leaders even notice him? When he entered Congress in April 1917, the short, youthful-looking New Yorker saw what he was up against. He was approached by House Speaker Joe Cannon, who called him "boy" and tried to get him to run an errand as if he were a congressional page, although he knew that Fiorello was a congressman. Cannon then faked surprise and said, "Oh, excuse me, I am not in the habit of seeing youngsters here as members." Cannon enjoyed this prank and repeated it more than once. But La Guardia was not daunted, and it did not stop him from voicing his views. On that first day, with his usual independence and boldness he marched into the House chambers and took one of the front seats, rather than sitting in back, as freshmen congressmen were expected to do. He even spoke up, which was unheard of for a newly minted representative.

La Guardia was to have more power than usual for a first-termer. The House was almost evenly divided between Democrats and Republicans, and therefore the five independents, which La Guardia was considered to be because he had run as a Progressive and a Republican, had considerable political strength. Although he had not yet fully developed his political philosophy, his resentment against the rich and his protective attitude toward the poor drew him toward the progressives in Congress. Eventually, he would become one of their spokesmen as their power decreased during the 1920s. La Guardia was also only the third Italian-American to be elected to Congress (the first in the twentieth century) and therefore not only spoke for the immigrant but also brought a needed "new" ethnic awareness to Republican progressives.

In Congress, Fiorello was thrust immediately into the discussions about U.S. entry into World War I. Unlike Robert La Follette and other antiwar western progressives, La Guardia by this time supported getting into the war. Many progressives thought the war served the big business interests and munitions dealers and therefore opposed entry. La Guardia, as a representative of the new immigrants, saw support of the war as an opportunity to assert his Americanism and that of the other new ethnics. In a period of increasing nativism, it was important to show that the new Americans were firmly behind the flag and as patriotic as old-stock Americans. He also saw the war as a way of breaking up the Austro-Hungarian empire and freeing its diverse nationalities. When Wilson called a special session of Congress for April 2, 1917 to ask for war, La Guardia, proclaiming his patriotism and portraying the war in humanitarian terms in regard to central Europe's various nationality groups, did not waver in his decision to vote in favor of Wilson's war message. It was also during his first days as a congressman that he proposed his bill to punish those who sold faulty supplies to the army. However, the bill failed to be reported out of committee.

He emerged during this first term as a independent-minded, concerned congressman who did his homework and understood the details of the bills coming up for a vote. He championed immigrant causes, challenging the premise of legislation that restricted immigration. He was, of course, against the Literacy Test Act, which required that potential immigrants be able to read in any language before entry was granted into the United States. He strongly opposed the Espionage Act of 1917, which allowed the government to punish those who made statements that were considered to interfere with the draft, enlistment, or the war effort in general, and to ban from the mails anything that was deemed disloyal.

Although upset about all these provisions, La Guardia questioned particularly the government's broadly stated right under the proposed act to curtail the printing of material that criticized any aspect of national defense. National defense was vaguely defined, and therefore La Guardia felt that this provision would limit press stories about abuses or inefficiency in the military system. Early on, La Guardia was a civil libertarian and fervently supported the Bill of Rights, which war hysteria now threatened. As he said, "The war to make the world safer for democracy must not serve as the pretext for the curtailment of the most essential freedoms." President Wilson tried to defend his proposals by maintaining that he would never really enforce the Espionage Act provisions to the extent that was causing concern. Events were to prove otherwise, and La Guardia did not want to take that chance anyway. He stated that "the law admittedly makes the president a despot, but with the comforting assurance that the despot about to be created has the present expectation to be a very lenient, benevolent despot. . . . The American people do not want tolerance; they demand the continuance of their constitutional rights." La Guardia won his point (although only temporarily, as indicated by the passage of the 1918 Sedition Act) on the provision regarding censorship of printed material. However, the Espionage Act, with all its other potentially abusive stipulations, passed in 1917. As a result, numerous Americans were soon to be arrested for simply criticizing the war, the Red Cross, or the Allies, or even just for supporting peace.

Fiorello was also disturbed by the Trading with the Enemy Act, which dealt with censorship of the foreign-language press and foreign communications and which gave the president the right to define the "enemy" broadly. La Guardia was again concerned about giving the president such power that he might arbitrarily designate individuals or various groups as "enemies," and thereby deny them their rights. Although Fiorello's colleagues did not accept his objections, nonetheless he remained a voice of reason during this period of burgeoning war hysteria. He understood, at this time, that during wartime a democracy's greatest enemy might be itself if it curtails freedom in the name of national security.

During La Guardia's early period in Congress, he served as the defender of the poor and downtrodden and as a spokesman for the foreign-born. His ethnic marginality, being American and Italian in culture, helped him serve as a broker between the immigrant and American worlds. He tried to explain to his constituents the necessity for the U.S. entry into the war and for a draft law and 100 percent support for the American war effort. To his congressional colleagues and government officials he defended the patriotism of the foreign-born. He also was quick to address the needs of the poor, speaking out on rising food prices, taxes on the lower classes, and postal rates. He thought that the war should not be waged to enhance corporate profits and benefit the wealthy. Distressed about the growing problems of the poor during a period of high prices and static wages, La Guardia felt that affordable food, housing, and clothing were rights that the government should ensure. Fiorello's concern for the poor was based not only on the needs of this group, but also on the needs of the nation, which he felt could not long survive if too many of its people lived a life of deprivation.

His style in Congress was aggressive, flamboyant, and boisterous; he had the ability to dramatize events and as a freshman congressman he often annoyed his more experienced colleagues. But the ambitious La Guardia needed the attention; he enjoyed being a showman and felt his causes were worth whatever was required to get them a hearing. He wanted people to know who he was, but he also knew he had to protect and defend the common people against selfish business interests and immigrants against self-satisfied and arrogant old-stock Americans. He spoke not only for his own New York constituents, but also for poor people across the nation. He disliked those whom he saw preying on the underprivileged, and was quick to attack greedy businessmen, bankers, corporation lawyers, and judges, who represented for him the people of wealth and influence who, he thought, had been responsible for his father's death.

The Great War

La Guardia was a man of conviction. If he voted for the draft bill, which would send other people to war, then he was willing to go himself as well. While the debate on the draft bill was proceeding in Congress, one of those opposing it asked its supporters whether they intended to serve. Fiorello was one of five who voiced his willingness to enter the armed forces. This decision was not out of character. La Guardia was familiar with military life, and he saw himself as a man of action. He also perhaps wanted to show that an Italian-American could be a good American patriot, and he felt morally obligated to stand with those who were to be drafted under a bill he had supported. Therefore, La Guardia readily joined the aviation section of the Army Signal Corps (there being no separate air force at the time) in July 1917.

Earlier, in anticipation of the possibility of war, La Guardia began taking flying lessons from Giuseppe Bellanca, brother of his union colleague and friend August Bellanca. Upon enlisting, La Guardia took a leave from Congress. He was made a lieutenant and prepared to embark for Europe for training, along with 150 aviation cadets. After arriving in Liverpool, these cadets were sent to British training schools and La Guardia (now a captain) and his commanding officer, Major Leslie McDill, were sent on to the Eighth Aviation Instruction Center in Foggia (the birthplace of Fiorello's father) with other cadets for training by the Italians. At Foggia the troops were under the command of Major William Ord Ryan. La Guardia was a good officer for his pilots but created many problems for his superiors. As always, he was independent, strong-willed, contemptuous of authority figures, and unlikely to follow orders he did not believe were suitable for his men.

Whether as a consular agent, an Ellis Island interpreter, a lawyer, a congressman, a soldier or a mayor, La Guardia

enjoyed taking care of those under his authority or less fortunate than himself. This attitude was not really related to
progressivism, although these concerns easily flowed into
the social welfare aspects of the Progressive movement;
rather it was part of La Guardia's innate desire to help, give
advice, uplift, and at the same time gain respect, wield
power, and snub his nose at authority. Shaped by his Arizona experience of seeing the powerless being taken advantage of, by his cultural marginality, which drove him to
crave status and power, and by his strong resentment of
those in control, Fiorello threw a protective arm around his
men and used his power on their behalf.

Two incidents indicate La Guardia's unique style as an
officer and his willingness to fight those in power. On one
occasion, one of Fiorello's men was killed in an aircraft that
La Guardia felt was unsafe. The United States had ordered
nearly one thousand of these planes from the Italian manufacturer. Even before the fatal accident, La Guardia had
complained to his superiors, to no avail, about the plane's
faulty design. Taking matters into his own hands, as he
often did, he went to the Italian manufacturer, said he was
the commanding officer of the American air forces in Italy,
and on his own authority abrogated the contract for the
planes. The Inter-Allied Purchasing Commission, which
had worked out the details of the contract, was aghast that
a mere captain had canceled the order and damaged
American-Italian relations. La Guardia was asked to come
to Paris to explain his actions. Without hesitation, he said
he canceled the planes to protect his men. Threatened with
dismissal, Fiorello responded by threatening to return to
the United States and go before Congress and the country
to ask why the army was buying unsafe planes. As a congressman, La Guardia could do that, and receive a lot of
publicity at the same time. The army relented, and the Italian government agreed that the planes were unsafe. Rather
than being dismissed or court-martialed, Fiorello was
hailed as an expert on aviation design and became the ar-

my's representative on the Joint Army and Navy Aircraft Committee in Italy, which dealt with the delivery of Italian planes. Eventually, La Guardia was put in charge of issues dealing with plane production in Italy.

The other incident involved securing decent food for his men at Foggia. Americans were getting the usual food served to the Italian troops, which La Guardia felt was inappropriate and insufficient for Americans. He therefore secured a better diet for his aviators by buying the food from a caterer. When the army quartermaster's office realized what was happening in Foggia, Fiorello was summoned to headquarters in Tours, France. An incensed general demanded that La Guardia explain his actions, threatening to bring legal charges against him for violating army regulations. La Guardia stayed calm. "Is that all that is troubling you, General?" La Guardia asked. "If so, I can have all that [the regulations] changed very easily." As La Guardia relates in his autobiography, "I thought the man would burst with rage. He pounded the desk violently, called me insolent, impertinent and demanded to know what I meant by saying that I could change Army regulations, which would take an act of Congress to accomplish." At this point, an aide informed the general that the target of his abuse was a member of Congress. He quickly calmed down, changed his attitude, and let Fiorello explain what had happened and what was needed. The general accepted the explanation and the matter was soon settled with discussions between La Guardia and his superiors in Paris. His men continued to receive their American-style food. Being a congressman had its rewards and it was clear that La Guardia had more authority than his captain's rank warranted.

During the war, La Guardia practically served as an ambassador to Italy. He delved into diplomatic issues, was on good terms with the Italian politicians, and toured Italy, giving effective and hard-hitting propaganda speeches on behalf of the war effort. He even wanted to travel to Switzerland to help organize a revolution with Hungarian exiles against their Austrian rulers, but President Wilson and the State Department refused to allow him to do so. Fiorello became well known in Italy and America and again served to bridge the European and American worlds. La Guardia also wanted to fight, although he could have had a non-combat job, and here too he fulfilled his desires with great bravado.

La Guardia admired Theodore Roosevelt, who was known for his heroic exploits during the Spanish-American War, and acted in much the same way. Fiorello excelled at physical heroism, both as a soldier during the bombing raids of World War I and later as a mayor, rushing into burning buildings. He enjoyed the publicity and excitement these exploits brought him and remained throughout his life an individual with both great personal courage and a desire to show it. During the war he went on bombing missions over the Austrian-Italian front, attacked Austrian targets, and faced enemy gunfire. His only war injury was from a crash during his first solo flight. Nonetheless, La Guardia was hailed as if he had beaten the Austrians single-handedly and had suffered numerous combat injuries during his heroic acts. The darling of the American press, decorated by the Italians, he returned to the United States on October 28, 1918, on leave from the army as the "flying congressman," a major, a hero, and a national figure. He did not resign from the Army until November 21, after the armistice. However, the major, as he now liked to be called for reasons of status, was not a hero to everyone at home.

"Why Doesn't He Go to Russia?"
The 1918 Campaign

La Guardia's congressional district had never been sold on the war. The Socialist party was strong in the area and many in the district were from the countries involved in the fighting and held various views on the American entry. Also, during his year in Europe La Guardia had not provided full-time attention to the needs of his constituents, and some were angry that they had been neglected while Fiorello achieved glory in far-off Italy. La Guardia had remained in Italy until late in his 1918 reelection campaign, and this too weakened his cause, although he was able to campaign even from Italy through the sympathetic American newspapers.

The main opponent in the Fourteenth Congressional District was the Socialist party's candidate, Scott Nearing, an economics professor. Nearing had consistently opposed the war, had suggested an early negotiated peace, and was under indictment under the Sedition Act of 1918 for an antiwar pamphlet he had written. He drew support not only from the Socialists, but also from many others who were dissatisfied with both La Guardia's absence and his support of the war. A petition drive already had been organized earlier under the slogan "Let's Be Represented" in an effort to get congressional approval to hold a special election for La Guardia's congressional seat because he was not fulfilling his duties. Fiorello's response, while still in Europe, was a good one that touched the nerve of patriotism. He commented, "I am now working not for my district, but for my country. You might say that if any signers of the petition will take my seat in a Caproni biplane, I shall be glad to resume my upholstered seat in the House." The tone of the coming campaign was set when La Guardia communicated from Italy in March that he would run on "an anti-yellow, anti-Socialistic, anti-German and true-blood American platform." La Guardia could be ruthless as a campaigner. He knew when and how to strike at his opponent's weak point, even though as an individual and a legislator he was not the divisive and overreacting zealot he sometimes appeared to be in campaigns.

Given the threat of the Socialist candidates and the patriotic fervor created by the war, the Republicans under New York County Republican chairman Sam Koenig and the Democrats under Tammany boss Charles Murphy decided to form a united front against the Socialists in vulnerable congressional districts and support the same candidates for Congress. La Guardia therefore received Republican and Democratic fusion backing in this campaign—the first and only time he was supported by Tammany—while in other districts the Republicans supported the Tammany choice.

Upon returning home, La Guardia launched into a clever campaign aimed at diminishing Nearing's substantial support by stressing the Socialist candidate's pacifism and obstructionism during the war. Fiorello's attacks on the Socialist party as well as its candidate were in some ways out of character, for he had worked closely with Socialists in the unions and during the 1920s was even to run with Socialist party support. But he had good issues to exploit in 1918 and he made the most of them.

He also campaigned in East Harlem's Twentieth Congressional District on behalf of his friend Isaac Siegel, also a Republican-Democratic fusion candidate running against a Socialist. Presaging the coming 1919–1920 Red Scare, La Guardia blasted away at the Socialists' lack of patriotism. By not supporting the war, he claimed, they had in effect collaborated with the kaiser. Part of this attitude stemmed from aggressive campaign tactics, and part from La Guardia's sincere belief that this was the war to end all wars and therefore had to be won. His attacks on Nearing continued. "If Scott Nearing wants to try out his beautiful theories," Fiorello proclaimed at one meeting, "why doesn't he go to Russia?"

In many ways, however, La Guardia agreed with the Socialists. Nearing attacked the greed of Wall Street, which La Guardia could certainly affirm. Yet La Guardia never was a Socialist and felt that the party was unrealistic in its reform thrust in that it would never attain sufficient political power to reform American society in the way it desired. And he maintained that Socialism had failed in Russia. La Guardia was too practical, too much of a realist, to accept the Socialist dream. He also did not want America's poor to wait in vain for that dream to be realized when so much needed to be done now. Fiorello felt that he was helping his district's poor and that they did not need the Socialists. He supported reform through unions, specific legislation, and change within the two-party system. Unlike some of his Italian friends, such as August Bellanca, and many Jewish constituents, who were attracted to Socialism because of its condemnation of worker exploitation and the abuses of the rich, La Guardia, although sharing their anger and desire for change, remained an independent and nominal Republican.

Given his seething resentments, perhaps if he had grown up in New York and seen the terrible exploitation of the workers and poor there, he would have taken a more radical course. But La Guardia was not a product of the city environment, did not spend his childhood in tenements and on crowded streets, and did not see his parents go off to work in sweatshops. He came to this world later, saw the grinding poverty of the immigrants and industrial workers, and related it to what he had seen in Prescott. He sympathized with the poor and realized the need for change, but wanted that change to take place within a capitalist framework. In this way he was more like Theodore Roosevelt and Robert La Follette, two of his heroes, than such Socialist leaders as Meyer London, who won election to Congress in 1914, 1916, and 1920, or Morris Hillquit, who helped found the Socialist party in 1901 and remained a major spokesman. He was also unlike Tammany politician Al Smith, who grew up in the slums but saw the Tammany machine as the vehicle for reform. Socialism or Tammany was the course for most immigrant slum dwellers in New

York who wanted to transform their urban environment. La Guardia, a westerner of middle-class background who viewed the Socialists as unrealistic and Tammany as hopelessly corrupt, forged his own reformist road in the Republican party. As such, he remained an oddity in New York politics, distinct from his generation of immigrant-stock Socialist and Democratic reform politicians. Although he was raised elsewhere, he was at home with native New Yorkers, immigrants, and the city's poor. They recognized that Fiorello was a sympathetic, outspoken ally who would fight for a better life for them.

Theodore Roosevelt saw himself as a moderate who was an essential alternative to the more radical elements. He envisaged the nation as heading for revolution unless moderates such as himself offered change within a capitalist structure. In some ways he was convinced that he had saved capitalism in the United States by offering a more mellow version of it through regulatory and social welfare concepts. La Follette, Norris, and Borah could make the same claims, as could La Guardia, who perhaps saw himself in this way. He was sure that he could offer the slum dwellers more than the Socialists in the way of realistic changes and improvements in their lives.

La Guardia won a strong victory over Nearing, beating him 14,523 to 6,214. The Socialists were defeated throughout New York City and La Guardia and other fusion candidates went to Congress. This was a good time in Fiorello's life: a stellar war record, an important political victory, and even marriage in March 1919 to Thea Almerigotti, whom he had courted for a few years.

His Voice Was Heard: Postwar Politics

The postwar period was a difficult time for the country. The nation was faced with reconversion to a peacetime economy, labor-management issues involving strikers, immigration, and concern over radicalism as well as Prohibition. In reaction against Wilson and the War, the United States was also entering a conservative era in which progressivism would be weakened and fragmented. The end of the Wilson years and into the 1920s required inspired leadership in Washington, which often was not forthcoming. La Guardia, although often not listened to, had an opinion on all matters. But during this postwar period his views on issues were not always consistent, as his political philosophy was still taking shape. His fervent patriotism and need to prove his Americanism drew him into the hysteria of the Red Scare. But his concern for civil liberties, his empathy for the downtrodden, and his hostility to bigotry pulled him in other directions. He joined with other progressives in Congress to urge the repeal of the Espionage Act during peacetime, sponsored a resolution to get the American representatives at the Paris Peace Conference to take an official stand against anti-Semitic incidents in Poland and elsewhere, opposed racial discrimination, rejected Prohibition, attacked corporate greed, supported the lower classes, criticized high food prices, and supported the League of Nations. He remained as hardworking as ever. Even on Sunday, when others relaxed, Fiorello kept at his congressional responsibilities, studying legislation and learning what each bill coming before the House said. Despite the fact that his work was his life, La Guardia cannot be considered a successful congressman at this time, because none of his bills became law. However, he spoke out on the issues frequently and loudly.

When the Eighteenth Amendment (establishing Prohibition) came up for vote in Congress in 1917, La Guardia, already in Italy, cabled his vote rejecting this addition to the Constitution. Through the 1920s, La Guardia was a leader in the fight against the prohibition of alcoholic beverages. He predicted correctly that it would not work and would cause more crime because ordinary people would show contempt for and violate the law. He felt that public education, not prohibitive legislation, was the answer to the drinking problem. Of special concern to Fiorello was the attack on the foreign-born that became part of the congressional debate on the Volstead Act in 1919, which provided for the enforcement of Prohibition and defined an alcoholic beverage. In leading the opposition to this bill, he defended immigrants against charges that it was their excessive drinking that was destroying the morals of the country. As he said in Congress in July 1919, "The greater majority of our working foreign element in this country have all they can do to buy proper clothing, shoes, and food for their families." Besides, they drank wine and beer rather than hard liquor and were not the source of the alcohol problem in the country. Instead, he suggested, the drinking problem lay with the native Anglo-Saxons. As he often did, he attacked the smug nativists who blamed all problems on the foreign-born.

Although La Guardia lost his legislative battles during the 1919–1920 congressional term, he was not overly concerned. Convinced that history would show that he had been on the side of right and justice, Fiorello doggedly pursued his convictions. La Guardia's determination to continue his battle with "the interests" made him at times overbearing, arrogant, and belligerent. These traits, combined with his independence, impatience, and disdain for authority, made it difficult for him to function effectively within a congressional system that valued diplomacy, seniority, and patience. Nobody forgot that he was around, though.

"The Town Isn't Ready for an Italian Mayor"

His congressional career was interrupted temporarily in 1919 when Republican leaders in New York urged him to run in a special election for president of the city's Board of Aldermen. This was a position that Al Smith had vacated the previous year when he won the governorship of the state. Although the Board of Aldermen presidency was usually a Tammany-held post, the Republican bosses thought that La Guardia looked like a winning candidate. He was popular, had good ties to Italians, Jews, and other immigrant-stock voters, was a war hero, and was a loud, if not powerful, voice in Congress. La Guardia ran for this local office largely based on his opposition to Wilson's peace treaty. By this time, Fiorello was angry that Italy had been denied the port of Fiume in the peace negotiations, and he therefore turned against Wilson's peace efforts, claiming that the president had "'blue-penciled' the . . . compromise regarding Fiume." There were other issues in the campaign, of course. For example, La Guardia also attacked Tammany's city leadership for its neglect of schools and the safety of school children. Nonetheless, the ethnic factor loomed large in this campaign. Many German-, Italian-, and Irish-Americans were dissatisfied with how their ancestral lands had been treated at the peace conference.

La Guardia initially had been unsure about the prospect of becoming aldermanic president and giving up his House seat. His political ambition was the deciding factor, because he had been promised, he claimed, the Republican nomination for mayor in 1921 if he did the party's bidding in 1919 and won. Fiorello began to think seriously about becoming mayor, a position of power from which he could help the underprivileged, achieve the respect and status he craved, and secure some representation for the immigrant groups for which he spoke. After all, Al Smith, another ethnic politician with strong reform inclinations, had jumped from president of the Board of Aldermen to governor.

On the basis of a strong anti-Wilson vote among ethnic voters in 1919, a number of Republicans won, including La Guardia, who beat the Tammany candidate, Robert L. Moran, in a close election. Supported by ethnics and good-government people (those who supported honest, efficient, machine-free government), La Guardia was able to become the first Italian to win a citywide post and the initial Republican to do so with the absence of fusion support from Democrats. He obviously was an effective vote getter and, as a rising star in Republican ranks, he fully expected to run for mayor in 1921. However, La Guardia was not the usual Republican and became more independent during the next two years—like Theodore Roosevelt, he was a politician the bosses had difficulty controlling.

He ran into problems with some in the party on a number of issues. He was outspoken against corporations, continued to defend the poor (siding, for example, with tenants against landlords), and attacked the Republican-dominated state legislature in 1920 for its ouster of five validly elected Socialist assemblymen. Most importantly, he strongly opposed Republican Governor Nathan L. Miller (elected in 1920 with La Guardia's help) because of the governor's support of Prohibition and immigration restriction, and his opposition to direct primaries for nominating candidates, New York City home rule, and social welfare legislation. The Republican leadership did not like Fiorello's independence and hostility, and his mayoral nomination in 1921 was in jeopardy.

But La Guardia used the aldermanic presidency, as he had his earlier positions, as a learning experience. He was one of two Republicans on the Board of Estimate. Made up of the mayor, the aldermanic president, the comptroller, and the five borough presidents, this board wielded the real power in the city because it controlled the budget, taxes, and contracts. The other Republican was Manhattan Borough President Henry H. Curran. La Guardia learned quickly the problems of New York and how the city operated. He gained a good grasp of transportation concerns, budget problems, and various educational, tax, and housing issues. He also began to develop a program for municipal reform that included a streamlining of city government through a new city charter. In all, he prepared himself to become mayor and sorted out some of his ideas on how best to run a city. He remained a tireless worker who worked late at night and then went out to make political speeches. When asked by a reporter what he did to relax, he replied that he worked.

It was during his two years as aldermanic president that La Guardia's independent streak and advocacy of social welfare created a rift with the state Republican leadership. Fiorello's views were simply not those of the party conservatives who were in power during the 1920s, but rather were those of the progressive Republicans. Although he worked with the party in the 1920 presidential election of Warren G. Harding and helped secure Italian-American votes, La Guardia's party loyalty was diminishing. He was convinced that the Republican party had to maintain its ties to the common people and help them if it was to stay in power. La Guardia increasingly was at odds with party positions as the 1920s wore on and as the power of progressives within the party diminished.

His opposition to Governor Miller and his growing independence on issues gave Fiorello some new press coverage. Called "a second Teddy Roosevelt" and "Champion of the People's Rights," La Guardia was now going off on his own, or at least increasing his identification with progressive Republicans and lashing out at the "stand-patters, reactionaries, and corporation-serving bosses of the party." He suggested the continuation of "the work of Theodore Roosevelt for a new school of politics." His position made him an unlikely Republican mayoral choice, and the party swung behind Henry Curran as their nominee in 1921, taking with them the support of anti-Tammany Democrats who backed a fusion ticket.

In a last-ditch attempt to secure the nomination, La Guardia decided to oppose Curran in the Republican primary. Party boss Sam Koenig warned Fiorello that "the town isn't ready for an Italian mayor," and noted later in the campaign that no promise of a mayoral nomination had been made to La Guardia. Fiorello nonetheless forged ahead. He used the campaign to speak out in favor of public housing, home rule, and good government. He also pitched his campaign to ethnics (particularly Italian-Americans) playing on ethnic pride, and women, pledging that he would bring them into his administration. However, without the Republican organization behind him, La Guardia lost to Curran in the September 1921 primary by a wide margin, even though he did well in Italian areas. Curran went on to lose to John F. Hylan, the Democratic incumbent.

Although he lost, La Guardia used the campaign as well as his aldermanic post to further develop his political ideas. His later mayoral positions on such issues as housing, transportation, and city charter revision can be traced to these years. Although previously he had fought for the poor and worked for good government, it was from 1920 to 1922 that La Guardia's ideas began to coalesce into a detailed, comprehensive progressive political agenda. It was also during this time that he began to identify his Republicanism with the tradition of Lincoln, La Follette, and Roosevelt. La Guardia saw this as a tradition of fighting greed, the monopolists, and "the interests" and supporting a government that "belongs to the people."

The Worst of Times

Fiorello's political defeat came at a time when his personal problems were mounting and each affected the other. This was a period of great personal tragedy.

During the winter of 1920–1921, La Guardia's wife, Thea, and daughter, Fioretta Thea (born in June 1920), were stricken with tuberculosis. He moved the family out of densely populated Greenwich Village to a private home he bought in a more open area in the Bronx. As his family's health deteriorated, Fiorello moved them to a rented house on Long Island. The baby was put in a nearby hospital. His wife subsequently was placed in a sanitarium in upstate New York. However, the disease could not be checked, and in May 1921 his baby died, followed by his wife in late November 1921. Between the two deaths, La Guardia himself was hospitalized because of a World War I injury that required an operation. While he was in the hospital, his Bronx house was robbed. To make matters even worse, his friend Enrico Caruso, the well-known operatic star, died in November. Fiorello went from his memorial service to Thea's deathbed; she died two days afterward. It was during this period of death and difficulty that La Guardia lost his primary election, and many considered him to be finished as a politician.

These tragic events may have led to La Guardia's foolish attempt to buck the Republican machine, almost as if he were not concerned with what the outcome would do to his political career. He had become angrier; his longstanding resentment against "the interests," against greed and corruption, had been exacerbated by the tragedy. He blamed New York's tuberculosis-ridden slum tenements for causing his family's death; now three people he loved (including his father) had died as victims of corruption and greed. These deaths further inspired La Guardia's zeal for social reform, which continued through his mayoral years. As he said shortly before leaving his aldermanic office in 1921, "New York is the richest city in the world. But until every child is fed and every home has air and light and every man and woman a chance for happiness, it is not the city it ought to be." Asked by a reporter whether he could do more with the city's substantial budget if he had the opportunity, La Guardia replied, "Could I! COULD I! Say! First,

I would tear out about five square miles of filthy tenements, so that fewer would be infected with tuberculosis like that beautiful girl of mine, my wife, who died—and my baby— I would establish 'lungs' in crowded neighborhoods—a breathing park here, another there. . . ."

CHAPTER THREE

"The Conscience of the Twenties"

After 1921, La Guardia, helped by his friends, began to rebuild his life at the age of forty. He went back into private law practice, taught, worked at organizing the Italian-Americans, and eventually restarted his political career. He was a wiser man, and was more determined than ever to do good for the people. He still was very ambitious, and was even surer of his ideological position.

La Guardia retained support in the Italian community, and he began to capitalize on that to rebuild his power. He created a personal support organization, the League of Italian-American Republican Clubs, that enabled him to appeal to the political yearnings of that group. It was clear that La Guardia, the city's most prominent Italian-American politician, would attract many who wanted to secure their group's equal place in New York's ethnic hierarchy. An ethnic politician who desired a comeback and supporters had found an ethnic group that needed a champion.

A Hard-Hitting Campaign

Based on his Italian support, some powerful press backing from millionaire publisher and maverick politician William Randolph Hearst, and articles he wrote for the *Evening*

Journal (a Hearst newspaper), La Guardia was able to make a quick move back into political office. After La Guardia threatened that he might challenge Governor Miller in the next election, in 1922 the leaders of the Republican party offered him a congressional nomination, which is what Fiorello wanted in the first place. An opening was found in East Harlem's Twentieth Congressional District and La Guardia agreed to run. This area was largely Italian with a substantial Jewish enclave, and was filled with the tenements of the working poor. It was a section that seemed ready-made for a La Guardia victory. He demanded that he be able to run his own race with his own program. Although a Republican, he would not be confined by the party platform. The Republican leaders reluctantly agreed in an effort to keep La Guardia out of the gubernatorial race.

Once again, as in the 1921 campaign, La Guardia was able to lay out his own ideas. He first revealed his platform planks when threatening to run against Miller and then discussed them further in his newspaper articles and during the congressional campaign. La Guardia made it clear that his Republicanism rested on progressive precepts. He supported minimum-wage legislation for women, old-age pensions, elimination of child labor, workmen's compensation, a law eliminating injunctions in labor disputes, rent control, city-owned housing, a change in the Prohibition laws to permit light wines and beers, a direct primary, a maximum eight-hour working day for women, public development of water-power sites, the initiative and referendum, equal political rights for women, and the end of a restrictive immigration system based on quotas and nationality. He also called for home rule for cities, a better credit system for farmers, the right of Socialists to free speech, the abolition of the state law censoring movies, elimination of teacher loyalty tests, a tax on land that increased in value while remaining unimproved (reminiscent of the Henry

George single-tax plan of the late nineteenth century), a bonus for World War I veterans, and the elimination of state income taxes for those earning less than $5,000 per year. Combining concepts from such earlier reformers as Henry George, as well as from the Populists, early progressives, municipal reformers, Socialists, and Theodore Roosevelt's 1912 insurgents, La Guardia was in tune, except on the Prohibition and immigration-restriction issues, with the western Republican progressives such as La Follette and Borah. He stood, as he said, for the Abraham Lincoln type of Republicanism and believed that the government's role was to support a fairer, more equitable industrial system. Clearly Fiorello, like Theodore Roosevelt before and Franklin Roosevelt after, was trying to save capitalism by reforming and humanizing the system.

La Guardia was a bridge between groups. He was the link between the western progressives and the machine-reform Democrats, such as Al Smith and Robert Wagner, who defended immigrant and working-class rights. He also connected the early Republicans and early Progressives with the reformers during the conservative 1920s. La Guardia sought to forge a party platform based on the concepts of Lincoln, La Follette, and Theodore Roosevelt. He saw Lincoln's ideas, for example, as an inspiration for his own on labor—ideas deemed radical by many in the party. Interpreting Lincoln, he concluded that the former president did not feel that government should exist for the protection of the wealthy. Thus, La Guardia felt that he, following in the tradition of Lincoln, was the true Republican, and that the others had drifted away from the founding precepts of the party. He could be pictured then as representing old values and an earlier generation of Republicans, but was using new techniques to achieve their goals.

La Guardia, along with other reformers of the 1920s decade, linked together the Progressive era with the New Deal. Surely, with his concerns for social welfare, public power, farm policy, and labor unions, his anti-Prohibition stand, his desire to forge a connection among various groups (e. g., immigrants and native-born Americans) to fight for social justice, and his support of the urban ethnics, Fiorello was practicing certain aspects of the New Deal long before it appeared on the national scene. La Guardia was therefore able to move easily into support of the New Deal later on. There were differences, of course, between the early La Guardia and the New Dealers on such issues as deficit spending, but Fiorello was a pragmatist who was willing to experiment to improve society. He became caught up in the experimentation of the New Deal and eventually accepted fully its fiscal policies. There were others, such as Wagner, who also served as links, but nobody else was able to represent so effectively the divergent elements of the progressive coalition and speak for those groups in the New Deal years. For immigrants, blacks, city dwellers, farmers, industrial workers, union members, and the poor, La Guardia was the link between the two great reform periods.

During the 1922 campaign, La Guardia won diverse support. Republican Senator Hiram Johnson of California, Theodore Roosevelt's vice-presidential candidate on the 1912 Progressive party ticket, backed him. He also received the endorsement of Democratic mayor Hylan, who had worked well with Fiorello when he was president of the Board of Aldermen and respected Fiorello's labors. As Hylan said, "La Guardia is the type of public official that renders service for the benefit of his constituents, regardless of political affiliations."

His opponents in 1922 were Democrat Henry Frank and Socialist William Karlin. Although La Guardia was more concerned about Karlin at first, he had already defused the Socialist threat by proclaiming himself a radical and a progressive (although still a Republican) and by developing a platform that would appeal to many Socialist voters. The greater threat came from the Democratic machine candidate, and La Guardia faced in this case a formidable opponent who knew how to run a hard-hitting campaign. The Frank campaign mailed a postcard to Jewish voters in the district that accused La Guardia of being anti-Semitic. However, by raising an ethnic issue, Frank was playing to La Guardia's strong point. Fiorello challenged his Democratic opponent, who was Jewish, to a debate to determine which of them was better able to serve all the people of the district, with the stipulation that the debate be in Yiddish. La Guardia was well aware that Frank did not speak Yiddish and thus could not participate. Frank, although he continued to accuse La Guardia of anti-Semitism, claimed that he was too ill to debate. La Guardia made a few speeches in Yiddish, stressing the absence of his opponent, and picked up some Jewish support.

The vote was close, but La Guardia won by 168 votes (8,492 for La Guardia, 8,324 for Frank, and 5,260 for Karlin). The closeness of the vote may have been the result of Tammany tricks, and La Guardia tried to keep an eye on the polling places. In some cases, as he had encountered before, Republicans worked against their own candidates. For example, La Guardia, just before election day, had been in a Republican leader's office when a Frank worker, not noticing La Guardia there, yelled "we've got the little wop licked! Here's your money." The Tammany machine was not beaten easily, even by the popular, multilingual Fiorello.

Republicans: A Party "Controlled by the Connivance of the Privileged Few"

From 1922 to 1932, La Guardia remained in Congress and forged a national reputation as one of the leaders of a small, vocal, and sometimes effective progressive bloc. He opposed the dominant conservatism of the 1920s, and particularly that ideological position within the Republican party. He spoke for the poor when the rest of the country was caught up in an excess of materialism and avarice and served, along with other progressives, in historian Howard Zinn's words, as "the conscience of the twenties."

Progressivism, although fragmented and out of power, played an especially important role during this time of business boosterism and corporate aggrandizement. Somebody was needed to reach out to those who were not part of the prosperity of the period, and to function as a check on the reigning conservative Republican politicians of the Harding, Coolidge, and Hoover years.

Progressives were, of course, active in Congress throughout this period. La Guardia fit nicely into this group when he won his House seat in 1922 and joined such senators as La Follette, Borah, Hiram Johnson, Irvine Lenroot of Wisconsin, Norris, and Thomas Walsh of Montana, and such congressmen as William Kvale of Minnesota and John Nelson of Wisconsin. Although Fiorello was the only progressive representative east of the Mississippi, he had always gotten along well with reformers whose roots, like his, were west of the Mississippi. As an indication of his political attitudes, La Guardia attended a conference of progressives (both politicians and others) in Washington, D.C., before the congressional session opened in 1923. The progressives were trying to marshal their forces to support reform legislation.

La Guardia returned to New York newly inspired by the progressive goal, noted at the conference, to eliminate the hold of special privilege on the government and to give the government back to the people. Soon after the meeting, Fiorello delivered a speech at a New York synagogue on "The Awakening of the Progressive Spirit in this Country" that lauded La Follette and urged a strong protest against monopolistic greed, government of and for the powerful, and exploitation of the people. He spoke of a coalition of industrial workers, farmers, and others organizing "against conditions which have become intolerable." The speech vented his long-held resentments against "the interests." In other speeches, he lashed out at the state Republican party, calling it a party "controlled by the connivance of the privileged few, for their benefit," and lambasted the reactionary elements in the party for their protection of monopolies against the interests of ordinary people. This was solid populist-progressive rhetoric. However, he did not agree with the progressives on all issues and remained hostile to their pro-Prohibition and anti-immigration positions. In that sense, La Guardia was a minority within a minority. Nonetheless, by 1923 he was one of the leaders of the Republican progressive group in the House, made up of midwesterners largely from Minnesota and Wisconsin. From 1923 through 1924, La Guardia took part in numerous meetings with other progressives to plan strategy and develop their legislative priorities. He was particularly helpful in joining the aspirations of rural and urban reformers by noting that their goals were the same. Like many progressives, La Guardia continued to admire La Follette, who he said was his "inspiration and ideal."

His independence from the regular Republicans continued to increase. Fiorello's voice was heard more and more in Congress as an advocate for the downtrodden and in support of progressive legislation. A flood of suggestions on social legislation, many already backed by La Guardia, poured forth from the congressman from the East Harlem slums during the next decade. La Guardia spoke out in favor of old-age pensions, urging both New York and the federal government to adopt them. The pensions, Fiorello claimed, would not be any more expensive than the poorhouses currently in use. He also supported such reforms as a shorter work week, unemployment insurance (as of 1930), aid to farmers, rent control, health insurance, regulation of food prices, and the abolition of child labor. In support of rent control, he told House members in April 1924 that "the right to live, the right to be sheltered, is just as necessary to the health and welfare, to the safety, of the community as the right to prevent disease, the right to prevent crime." Child labor was of particular concern to him, and he tried to get an amendment to the United States Constitution that would eliminate industry's abuse of children. His concern for children was sincere and emotional. On one occasion he left a sickbed against his doctor's orders to vote in favor of an amendment regulating child labor. La Guardia thought of himself as a father and protector to the less fortunate, especially children, who he felt should receive his special attention. Not only did child labor exploit children and keep them out of school, but it also gave an unfair competitive edge to states that allowed it by enabling their industries to pay lower wages than adults would receive and, of course, preventing unions from gaining a foothold. He maintained a strong interest in this issue throughout his political career, and later as mayor used the Juvenile Aid Bureau of the city's police department to eliminate child labor violations.

He continued to speak out aggressively against corporate greed and favored a higher income tax on the rich. He was not an idealist seeking utopia, but instead a practical but concerned politician who wanted the system to work efficiently and fairly for all, not just the privileged few. So far, the 1920s prosperity had not helped his East Harlem constituents, and thus he did not accept the administration's idea that what was good for business was good for all Americans. La Guardia maintained that the Republican party was headed for destruction unless it became more concerned with the people and less with the holders of power and wealth. Fiorello's thinking is reminiscent of that of Theodore Roosevelt who had worried about class conflict or even a revolution if the Republican party and the courts did not respond to the needs of the growing number of discontented workers and underprivileged in the country and curb the exploitive business methods of some corporations. In 1900, about 40 percent of the U.S. population existed below the poverty line. Although conditions had certainly improved by the 1920s, there still were many Americans who were not enjoying that era's prosperity.

To pay for new social programs, La Guardia suggested an increase in taxes on corporations. Corporate taxes, as well as income and inheritance taxes on the wealthy, would not only provide revenue, but also avert the amassing of great wealth by only a few people. Many reformers saw the concentration of wealth as a danger to democracy, giving the rich too much power over government and the economy. Fiorello was far from alone in his concern over concentrated wealth; it had long been a populist-progressive issue. La Guardia carried on the fight begun by such notable progressives as William Jennings Bryan and Robert La Follette. He was also, of course, speaking for his own constituents, who had little in common with the country's rich industrialists and financiers. By the time of the Depression (and as part of Fiorello's long opposition to Marxism for offering unrealistic goals), he felt his social legislation would eliminate any attraction communism had for the poor. As he said, "This is my answer to Communism—to remove the cause of complaint, to take away the argument of the agitator and do something that will make life easier and better for the great masses of the working people of this country."

Fiorello's policies, which were similar to those of other progressives, put him in direct opposition to President Calvin Coolidge and Secretary of the Treasury Andrew Mellon. Their program favored big business and the wealthy with tax breaks, a high tariff, hostility to unions, and lax regulation. The glorification of business that characterized this decade and prompted Coolidge to say that "the business of America is business" was anathema to the remaining progressives. These reformers maintained their long-held antipathy toward the power of the corporations.

La Guardia believed that the real geniuses of the country were not the Morgans and Mellons but the common people such as his hard-working, but poor constituents. As he wrote in 1928, "can any one of them [millionaires such as Mellon] improve on the financial genius of Mrs. Maria Esposito or Mrs. Rebecca Epstein or Mrs. Maggie Flynn who is keeping house in a New York tenement, raising five or six children on a weekly envelope of thirty dollars a week, paying thirty and twenty-five dollars a month rent, trying to send the children to school warmly clad and properly nourished, paying exorbitant gas and electric bills and trying to provide meat at least once a day for the family?" Challenging the pervasive belief in Social Darwinism that was evident in the late nineteenth century and again in the 1920s, La Guardia proclaimed the superiority of the working poor over the avaricious rich.

His hostility to the financial policies of the Harding-Coolidge years which emphasized aiding the rich and allowing prosperity to trickle down to the poor, was evident in his opposition to Mellon's tax plan. Like William Jennings Bryan in his "Cross of Gold" speech at the 1896 Democratic convention, La Guardia felt that a better idea for government would be to allow prosperity to trickle up—to enrich society by making the masses more prosperous. Although Fiorello supported the balanced budget advocated by the administration, he opposed tax reforms that favored the wealthy. From the beginning of his tenure under Harding, Mellon had pushed for a tax cut on the higher brackets as a way to spur investments and stimulate the economy. Specifically, in a plan introduced in 1923, Mellon proposed a decrease in the surtax on high incomes from 50 percent to 25 percent, along with some minor reductions for the lower tax brackets. La Guardia blasted this idea on the floor of the House, stating that high taxes on the wealthy must be preserved as a way of preventing the accumulation of huge wealth by a few, wealth that encouraged more greed and led to scandals such as Teapot Dome. As La Guardia said in Congress in February 1924:

> the danger of the concentration of enormous fortunes in a few hands is quite obvious—we are now witnesses to a national scandal, the result of enormous fortunes. A great deal has been said here about releasing money for business, for new developments, for new enterprises. "Reduce taxes and encourage business" is the slogan. . . . Men with enormous fortunes and large incomes do not release their money on hazardous new enterprises. They let others do it and then come in. This country was developed before we had large fortunes. It is after the development became successful and exploitation set in that your large fortunes are made. . . . So I do not see much in the argument that you are going to release money for new enterprises if you reduce the taxes.

The Mellon tax plan passed nonetheless, in altered form, resulting in a bill that placed a 40 percent surtax on high incomes and raised the inheritance tax. However, the surtax on the higher incomes had been lowered from 50 percent—a triumph for the wealthy.

Although La Guardia gained little support for his proposals during a decade when wealth was worshiped and materialism reigned supreme, he hoped at least to raise certain issues and educate the public. Therefore, he continued his fight for the underdogs of society. When Mellon in 1925 and again in 1927 proposed further tax cuts for the rich and an elimination of the inheritance and gift taxes, La Guardia rose again in the House to offer his opposition. But his objections did little good, and Mellon's tax cut plans passed.

La Guardia grew increasingly disillusioned with the Republican party, which he felt now existed for the benefit of the rich and big business and had drifted from its Lincoln-Roosevelt base. Many Republicans, in turn, began to see him as someone they no longer could back. The break had been coming for some time. By early 1924 La Guardia identified himself, not as a Republican, but as a member of the House progressive bloc. This group urged adoption of tax cuts for the poor, regulation of child labor, aid for farmers, control of labor injunctions and government supervision of the basic needs of life, such as food and fuel.

A Progressive Resurgence?

In 1924 progressives met in Cleveland, drawing together diverse reform elements, ranging from Jacob Coxey (who had led a march on Washington in 1894 to demand a public works program for the unemployed) to supporters of the Populists, Socialists, Greenbackers, and single-taxers, to Wilson, Roosevelt, and La Follette progressives. La Guardia was a leading figure at the meeting, proclaiming, as he had already done at an East Harlem gathering, that he would "rather be right than regular." The progressives, in rejecting both the Coolidge-Mellon "prosperity" of the Republican party and the conservative swing of the Democrats (who eventually selected Wall Street lawyer John Davis as their candidate in 1924), formed a new Progressive party that nominated Robert M. La Follette for president and Democratic Senator Burton K. Wheeler for vice-president. The platform borrowed much from the reform ideas of the Populists and 1912 Progressive party, and also included 1920s concerns. The new party called for laws that would guarantee the right of workers to unionize and that would bar labor injunctions; advocated limits on court review of legislation; supported the election (rather than appointment) of judges; and sought the implementation of an initiative and referendum process on the federal level, a lower tariff, a provision for a national referendum before war could be declared, government ownership of the rail-

roads, the direct election of the president, and other reforms. Many of La Guardia's ideas had indeed found a political home.

Despite his rhetoric, La Guardia had not yet officially
split with the Republican party or even decided that he
would do so. Republican boss Sam Koenig was well aware
of La Guardia's indecision as well as his vote-getting abilities and was averse to losing him as a Republican, although
there were other Republicans who wanted to kick La Guardia out of the party. Koenig offered Fiorello the backing of
the party in 1924 for his reelection as congressman if La
Guardia would throw his support to Coolidge and remain
a regular Republican. La Guardia then made his decision
to break with the party and added that he could not "sacri-
fice principle for the sake of a party nomination or anything else." He concluded his answer to Koenig by noting
that "Theodore Roosevelt set the example of righteousness
rather than regularity" in 1912. This was a bold move; rejecting the Republicans meant losing his usual organizational support. However, La Guardia's public and noisy
spurning of a Coolidge ticket and the Republican platform
would not hurt him in East Harlem. This was a case where
ambition and principle could neatly merge. La Guardia
was strongly opposed to what he called "the reactionary attitude of the Republican majority" in the House, and was
unwilling to support a candidate whom he felt was detrimental to the country and to his district. Securing the support of Progressives and Socialists, La Guardia could satisfy
both his ambitions and his beliefs, and maintain his independence.

The 1924 election pitted La Guardia against Democrat
Henry Frank, his 1922 opponent, and Republican Isaac
Siegel, the former congressman of the district. In this election, Fiorello ran not only on the Progressive party line but
also secured the endorsement of the Socialist party, al-

though he clearly was not a Socialist. The Socialists backed him because they wanted to put Progressives into office and perhaps create a new coalition reform party. La Guardia did not have a difficult time in this campaign, because he had strong support from union and Italian groups, from his friends and ideological allies. He also pulled the ethnic strings of his district well, lashing out at immigration restriction, lambasting the anti-Semitic Henry Ford, condemning the British jailing of Irish independence leader Eamon De Valera, and, as always, offering himself as a symbol of the Italian political coming-of-age. Finishing his campaign at what became his lucky corner, 106th Street and Lexington Avenue, the Progressive-Socialist candidate was poised for a big victory in the midst of 1920s conservatism.

As expected, La Follette lost the presidential race substantially, carrying only one state (Wisconsin), whereas Coolidge took 54 percent of the national vote. But in the Twentieth Congressional District, La Guardia was triumphant, with 10,756 votes to Frank's 7,141 and Siegel's 7,099. La Guardia was the only Progressive elected in the East, but was classified, over his objections, as a member of the Socialist party when he took his seat in the House. In some ways it was an empty victory. Fiorello was left without any power in the House, because he was no longer a Republican, and was denied any important committee assignments. He continued to fight loudly and strongly for his causes, but he also eventually looked again for Republican party support for his campaigns.

At first, he tried to maintain the viability of the Progressive party in his district, although nationally the party was dead by 1925. With a coterie of personal followers, he was able to develop and maintain a Progressive club in his area, separate from the Republican machine. Other Progressive congressmen who had split from the Republicans also faced a weakened organizational structure. Could they stay in office while constantly bucking the two major parties and without the financial support and congressional committee assignments available to a regular party member? Theodore Roosevelt had moved back into the Republican party after his insurgency in 1912; many progressive Republicans would do the same. La Guardia kept his ties with other former Progressive party supporters, and in 1926 even suggested that the United States needed a realignment of the two major parties to create separate conservative and progressive organizations—an idea he would reiterate in the 1930s.

Still maintaining his independence and hoping for a revival of the Progressive party, La Guardia also realized as a practical politician that this third party was gone. He was willing to run in 1926 as an independent. But he found that the Republican party wanted to nominate him. Eager for the Republicans' organizational support for his campaign and the good committee assignment in Congress that the Republican label would bring, Fiorello agreed to rejoin the party and run as its candidate. As for the party, there was no mystery about its wish to bring La Guardia back into the organization. Fiorello would draw voters, particularly ethnic ones, to the Republicans.

In a close election in 1926, Fiorello beat the Tammany candidate, H. Warren Hubbard, and became the Republican party's sole victor in the city's congressional races. It was a Democratic year; Al Smith was reelected governor and Robert F. Wagner went to the Senate. The Democrats used various tactics, including violence, to try to defeat La Guardia. But he fought back hard, kept a close watch on the polling places, and managed to outmaneuver Tammany. For his efforts, La Guardia received a position on the important House Judiciary Committee. La Guardia remained nominally a Republican and continued to secure the party endorsement in subsequent congressional elections. However, he also continued to criticize the Republicans and stayed as an independent voice in Congress.

An Odd Political Makeup

La Guardia also directed criticism at foreign policy and defense issues. He temporarily followed the isolationist position of La Follette and other progressives and drifted from his prowar stand of World War I days. He thus opposed American intervention in a Nicaraguan revolution in 1927. Positive that greedy and evil business interests fomented wars for economic purposes, he objected to the use of American forces in Latin America or elsewhere at this time. He also, in 1928, began to question the nation's priorities in defense and domestic spending. Fiorello asked, when speaking before Congress, "Do you realize that you are living in a country that spends 70 percent of its entire expenditures for past, present and future wars?" He suggested that the money would be better spent on children. Understanding the irony of his society, La Guardia went on to state that when he returned from the war he was feted as a hero because he "had dropped bombs; but when I went down to City Hall and tried to appropriate more money for milk and better homes for these children—then they called me a 'Radical!'" The eager soldier of World War I had begun to see the broader picture of what threatened the future of the country.

He still felt the Republicans were not answering the needs of the American people, particularly those in his district, and urged a less conservative program. In 1928 he refused to endorse Herbert Hoover, the Republican candidate for president. However, the party continued to back La Guardia, and he easily defeated the Democrats' candidate, Samuel J. Dickheiser. The 1930 contest, with the Great Depression already beginning, saw the Republican

La Guardia face Vincent Auleta, Tammany's first Italian-American candidate, for this congressional seat. The Democrats were slowly opening the doors to Italians in an effort to win the ethnic vote, but Fiorello took the race by a healthy margin.

After his 1928 victory, Fiorello married his long-time secretary and advisor, Marie Fischer, on February 28, 1929. They later adopted two children, Jean in 1932 and Eric in 1934. True to his work habits, Fiorello even on his wedding day rushed back to his congressional office after the ceremony. His work, as always, came first.

In Congress La Guardia continued to maintain an independence that set him apart, not only from Republicans, but also from other progressives. It is this maverick capacity that best reveals La Guardia's odd political makeup. He was a progressive who was generally in tune with his ideological cohorts in the West and Midwest, but he also had much in common with Tammany men such as Al Smith, who represented the immigrant-stock population. On some issues, La Guardia was clearly in the western Republican progressive camp, reflecting his western, anti-Tammany upbringing and reform interests. On other issues, he was with the representatives of the immigrant slums, based on his second-generation Italian-American background and ethnic concerns. Fiorello represented two American traditions, western populism-progressivism and urban immigrant-based reform. He therefore often displeased one or the other group when they were in conflict, as with Prohibition and immigration restriction.

Prohibition, passed into law as the Eighteenth Amendment to the U.S. Constitution in 1919, was supported more in rural areas than in cities. In the countryside, Protestant fundamentalism and the connection of drinking and sin spurred the movement to eliminate alcohol. Rural, old-stock Protestant Americans, largely in the southern and western states, were the driving force behind the "Great

Experiment." Progressives such as La Follette, who represented the rural states and an older America, while declaring against Prohibition, voted for it in the Senate. No such uncertainty existed for urban immigrant spokesmen such as Smith, Wagner, or La Guardia. In the cities, where fundamentalism held little sway, Prohibition was unpopular. As already noted, Fiorello had attacked Prohibition by opposing the Eighteenth Amendment and the Volstead Act. Various aspects of Prohibition troubled him—the power of the government to impose morals, the capability of the rich to bypass the law through payoffs as well as by stocking up on liquor before the law went into effect, and the violation of civil liberties by overzealous police. To both show his contempt for the Volstead Act and demonstrate how easy it was to violate, Fiorello announced in 1926 that he would make beer using legally obtained ingredients. First in the room where the congressional Committee on Alcoholic Liquor Traffic met and later in a drugstore in East Harlem, with the press in attendance, La Guardia mixed legal near beer with legal malt tonic, which contained alcohol, to produce real, illegal beer. The newspapers had a good time with this story, and the "La Guardia formula" for making beer became known across the nation. As a result, New York's Prohibition office warned that anybody making beer this way would be arrested. This warning prompted Fiorello to make his beer in the East Harlem drugstore, daring the police to arrest him. They refused.

Although La Guardia could not get Prohibition repealed during the 1920s, he hoped to indicate how foolish it was, especially since illegal real beer could be made from two legally bought products. Fiorello was not one to break the law, but he felt this law was wrong, that it needlessly wasted government funds that could be used for better causes and bred disrespect for laws in general. He also pointed out how ridiculous it was to try to patrol the borders with so few Prohibition agents. He suggested that either sufficient money be made available to enforce Prohibition, or that it should be repealed. But he knew that no amount of funding could enforce Prohibition. Fiorello commented that "bootleg whiskey, hootch, moonshine . . . are sold within a stone's throw of the Prohibition Headquarters in Albany [New York]. Everybody but the prohibition unit knows that Albany is wide open and that all the hootch desired can be obtained by simply going up and asking for it." Prohibition was simply not working, and La Guardia, ever the showman craving attention, was able to publicize the foolishness of making alcohol illegal after it had been legal for so long.

Immigration restriction was a more serious issue for La Guardia. To say that Italians or other "new immigrant" Americans did not make good Americans and therefore should be denied entry into the country was a personal insult to him. In a decade when the Ku Klux Klan was a powerful organization, Al Smith's religion was attacked during the 1928 presidential campaign, Henry Ford's *Dearborn Independent* promoted anti-Semitism, and Nicola Sacco and Bartolomeo Vanzetti were convicted for murder and went to the electric chair based on their radical beliefs and Italian background, all "new immigrant" groups were under siege. The nativism of old-stock Americans, along with the unions' concern about too many workers coming to the United States and depressing wages, fueled the immigration restrictionism of this era. Once again urban ethnic representatives in Congress were generally opposed to curtailing immigration, whereas those from rural-based, old-stock states and districts supported it. The progressives with whom La Guardia worked so closely on other issues— La Follette, Borah, Wheeler, and Norris—either supported restriction outright or refused to take a stand on the issue. In either case, they did not see the immigrants as their concern. La Guardia was a vigorous, outspoken, and dedicated opponent of restrictionism based on religion, race, or national origin, viewing it as bigoted and inspired by a false sense of Anglo-Saxon superiority.

Seeing the immigration restriction acts as the work of

small minds that defined an "American" in the narrowest terms, La Guardia kept up a steady barrage against the legislation, even after the Johnson-Reed (National Origins) Act was passed in 1924. As he said in Congress before the bill was passed, "You can not escape the responsibility of the vicious, cruel discrimination against Italians and Jews mainly, along with the other countries I have named, which you make in the bill you propose to support." Fiorello also asserted that all he has heard in the House was "expressions of fear for the future of the Republic unless we slam the door in the face of races which have a thousand years of civilization back of them and open the doors only to Anglo-Saxon stock." But given the temper of the times, he managed to convince few in Congress. Fiorello did acknowledge that a limit on immigration as a result of a declining economy was acceptable as a way to safeguard American workers. But he rejected a curb on immigration based on other than economic factors, restrictions that gave preferences to so-called superior ethnic groups. Fiorello's support of the urban ethnics, his defense of their value to the country, and his ties to progressivism presaged the New Deal coalition. So did La Guardia's defense of blacks. He supported federal funds for Howard University and equal opportunity in education and he attacked Jim Crow actions, even though few blacks lived in his congressional district. In his advocacy of urban ethnics and the rural population, workers and farmers, and the poor of all races, La Guardia developed an ideological appeal that Franklin Roosevelt's New Deal would refine.

"The People Will Survive"

When the Great Depression struck the country after the 1929 stock market crash, La Guardia's views on poverty, government aid, and unions were redeemed. His warnings about Coolidge-Mellon economic policies that aided the

wealthy and did little for poor industrial workers or farmers proved accurate. As the depression deepened in sever-
ity, the country recognized the correctness of what La
Guardia had been saying all along. The establishment of a
system in which 5 percent of the population controlled
about 33 percent of all income, and in which tax breaks
gave that wealthy 5 percent the means to invest in the stock
market and send it to grossly inflated highs, was detrimental to the economic health of the nation. High tariffs supported by the Republicans during the 1920s restricted
other countries from selling their products here. As a result, they had difficulty paying the United States back for
loans and purchasing American goods. A poorly regulated
consolidation of American business allowed corporations
to wield too much political and economic power. La Guardia now pushed to secure his reforms.

Long a friend of unions, even taking his turn on picket
lines in various strikes, Fiorello had wanted to prevent federal courts from ordering striking workers back to work or
barring strikes. He also sought to secure the right of workers to unionize and bargain collectively. Judges, who
tended to be favorably disposed toward corporations, easily and often destroyed union power and workers' hopes
for an equitable settlement by issuing injunctions against
strikes. La Guardia's efforts, along with those of Senator
Norris, culminated in the passage of the Norris-La Guardia
Act in March 1932. The act offered the following provisions: it eliminated injunctions against strikes (except in
cases where the boss could show that he had made a sincere
effort to end the strike, or that the workers had threatened
him, or that the strike would ruin his business); it acknowledged the right of trial by jury for those accused of violating an injunction; it made yellow-dog contracts (an
employer-induced stipulation that a worker would not join
a union while at that job) not legally enforceable; and it
acknowledged that workers had the right to unionize and

bargain collectively. This act was a major victory for labor and served as the forerunner of sections of the National Industrial Recovery Act of 1933 and the National Labor Relations Act of 1935 during the New Deal period. It was perhaps Congressman La Guardia's finest moment and the legislation for which he is most remembered. Workers now had rights to organize, bargain, and strike. And the act made the federal courts remain impartial on labor-management issues, instead of portraying the strong pro-employer bias of previous years.

La Guardia was an active legislator during the depression's economic collapse, spurred on by letters from constituents and those outside his district that spoke of the growing misery in the country. Fiorello was convinced that immediate action had to be taken to alleviate the public's distress. And he was sure it could be alleviated. As he said, "There is no more justification for unemployment in this day and age than there is for epidemics of preventable diseases." He proposed various measures to deal with the depression, such as unemployment insurance, an expanded public works program (including the building of public housing), federal insurance of savings bank deposits, food and other relief aid, and abolition of child labor, a reform he had suggested earlier. Working with other progressive-minded individuals who reacted to the nation's problems, such as senators Wagner, Norris, and Borah, La Guardia pushed for various ways to help the urban and rural poor and to relieve mass suffering. He wanted the government to respond to the needs of the people and to understand that recovery would only take place when the working class received fair treatment from business and government and a fair share of the economic pie. Although President Hoover supported public works programs, he would not listen to the calls for increased government spending or direct federal relief aid for those out of work. The president was concerned with limiting federal government interference in the economy and feared creating a citizenry that was too dependent on the federal government. Hoover was also unwilling to accept fully the reports about the disastrous impact the economic collapse was having on the country.

La Guardia and other progressives also clashed with Hoover on the issue of public ownership of power sites. This issue went back a number of years. During World War I, the government had begun to build a large munitions-manufacturing complex at Muscle Shoals, Alabama, on the Tennessee River, that contained a hydroelectric plant and nitrate plants. After the war, the complex remained a potential source of electric power and nitrogen fertilizers for farmers. For years the business-oriented federal government of the 1920s had sought to lease this property to private businessmen (initially Henry Ford) and had been opposed by progressives, particularly Senator Norris and Congressman La Guardia. Both reformers preferred to have the federal government continue to control this operation, develop dams for flood control, and sell inexpensively both electric power and fertilizer to improve life in the Tennessee Valley area. As La Guardia saw it, the idea of leasing the property to Henry Ford made the Muscle Shoals bill (which authorized such a lease) "a bill to make Henry Ford the industrial king of the United States."

The thrust of the progressive interest in Muscle Shoals fit very well with the goals of some earlier progressives, who desired public ownership of natural resources such as oil, gas, and water. Conservatives saw this reform plan as a major step into socialism. Norris urged the government to become involved in the electric power industry and construct and run power projects across the nation. Muscle Shoals, La Guardia believed, could serve as proof that the government rather than private industry should handle public utilities. "Every big financial interest . . . ," he said in Congress, "that has been opposing the municipal operation of electric power and heat and water plants and all the railroads are hoping you will pass this bill [to lease the property to Ford] in order to stop the future development of Government operation of public utilities. You are putting back the progress of government 100 years by presenting this bill and passing it." Although the bill passed the House, it was blocked in the Senate. Fiorello continued to believe that government should serve the people and make their lives better and was suspicious of private industry reaping enormous profits from and controlling a basic need and a natural resource.

Through the Coolidge and Hoover years, La Guardia pushed unsuccessfully for continued government control and development of Muscle Shoals. Nonetheless, the efforts of Norris and La Guardia eventually bore fruit in the 1933 New Deal creation of the Tennessee Valley Authority. This agency served not only to develop electric power in the region, but also to use its lower rates as a yardstick by which to determine fair rates for the private utility companies. La Guardia again foreshadowed the New Deal.

La Guardia's suspicion of the rich and their wielding of power at the expense of other classes in society contributed to his antipathy to leasing Muscle Shoals to private enterprise. The depression, which seemed so clearly to many people to have been caused by avarice and stupidity on the part of wealthy investors, business moguls, and their rich political allies, gave La Guardia the opportunity to strike back at these groups. Angry at what they had done to the country, he wanted to ensure that it could not happen again. Also, he was concerned about a budget deficit that would grow as the government's antidepression efforts increased and tax monies decreased. He warned that "we must not pass on to future generations the burden of paying for the failures, the blunders, the mistakes of our present financial collapse," and along with other progressives, he pushed for higher taxes on the wealthy. La Guardia believed that the rich, not the poor, should pay (in taxes) for the mistakes that led to the depression. He aggressively led the fight against a 1932 sales tax to raise revenue, which would disproportionately affect the poor. Instead, Fiorello proposed to raise taxes on incomes of $100,000 and over, stock transfers, safe-deposit boxes, and luxury purchases. In a sharp reversal of policy in March 1932, in part brought on by La Guardia's pressure and the increasing public disgust with the wealthy, Congress voted down the sales tax and voted in various taxes on the rich that Fiorello had proposed.

La Guardia also supported more regulation of the stock market, which would require companies to provide quarterly reports and other information so as to prevent the sale of worthless stock. (Once again La Guardia foresaw what would later be a component of New Deal policy with the Securities and Exchange Commission.) He further opposed any legislation, such as a bill establishing the Reconstruction Finance Corporation and a Federal Home Loan Bank Act, that would aid the nation's bankers at a time when the government was doing little to alleviate the financial distress of common people. La Guardia, outraged, maintained that there should be "no dole for the millionaires! The bastards broke the People's back with their usury and now they want to unload on the government. No. No. No. Let them die; the People will survive." La Guardia was sincerely concerned about the large number of foreclosures taking place and the unfair interest rates being charged. He wanted to protect homeowners and railed against bankers' greed as one way to dramatize his concerns. After the passage of the Federal Home Loan Bank bill, he secured an amendment limiting the interest rates banks could impose on mortgages and other loans. The large amount of mail he received from distressed homeowners and others who supported his position in regard to the bankers indicated that La Guardia spoke for the people and their needs. A people's lawyer in his early days, he was also a people's congressman.

A Tammany Victory

Nowhere was this more evident than in his home district. La Guardia tried to take care of his constituents' needs, although his interest in national problems took more and more of his time as the depression crisis worsened. One story related by Ernest Cuneo, his law clerk and friend, indicates how Fiorello operated. One winter night in 1932, a man from La Guardia's district walked into his office complaining that the gas had been turned off in his apartment and that his children were suffering from the cold. The individual, poorly dressed for the winter and obviously down on his luck, asked La Guardia for help. Fiorello, as he often did, was willing to contribute his own money, but went further than that. After finding out that the gas had been turned off without any notice from the company, La Guardia called the governor's office, although it was late, secured the home telephone number of the public service commissioner, and phoned him. He blasted the commission and the gas company, and warned that he would begin investigations in Congress unless something was done to help this unfortunate man and his family. The gas company soon sent out an emergency crew, which quickly restored the gas to the man's apartment. La Guardia took similar action many other times. Angered by the suffering he witnessed in his district, he consistently tried to help people who had to deal with unconcerned bureaucrats and with unfeeling company officials who worried only about the financial bottom line.

Helping him in his district and actually managing his campaigns and developing his organization was another second-generation Italian-American, Vito Marcantonio, who later became a congressman from this same area. La

Guardia first met Marcantonio in 1921 when Vito was a high school student. Favorably affected by an address Marcantonio presented to a school assembly on Social Security and old-age pensions, La Guardia eventually began helping the youngster in his career, spoke of him as his "professional heir," brought him into his law firm, and put him in charge of his operations in the district.

Marcantonio became a lawyer and, like La Guardia, was concerned with injustice in society and the plight of the poor, and devoted his life to dealing with these problems. He became a neighborhood activist involved in tenants' rights, immigrant issues, and other social causes. Like his mentor, Marcantonio was hostile to "the interests," desirous of political power, and effective as a hard-hitting multilingual campaigner. But unlike Fiorello, Marcantonio had been raised in the poverty of New York's mean streets. He saw it all firsthand and had been attracted, not to the Republicans, but to the Socialists and their zeal for economic and social reform. Although Marcantonio tied his career to Fiorello's and came under his influence, the younger man remained much more radical, as was shown by his congressional career and the strong support he received from Communists.

Marcantonio became La Guardia's link to a younger generation of reformers who would continue Fiorello's efforts in his district. In 1924 Marcantonio joined La Guardia's campaign for Congress as his campaign manager, and later continued the 1924 campaign structure in the F. H. La Guardia Political Club, an entity that was distinct from the Republican organization, which La Guardia did not trust. By the 1930s, club members were called *Ghibboni* (gibbon apes), a name that they jokingly gave themselves. These *Ghibboni* were Fiorello's front-line troops and were responsible for organizing, under Marcantonio's tutelage, support for La Guardia in the district. The club was largely made up of Italian-Americans, both immigrant and second-generation, which indicated La Guardia's influence on both groups. Many young Italian-Americans wanted to move up in life and saw politics as their ladder to success, and they joined the club as a way to achieve their goals. Tammany was still viewed, correctly, as doing relatively little to enhance Italian aspirations. La Guardia, however, was their link to status and political power. Certainly, Marcantonio used the club and La Guardia to secure his own political aims.

The club had another function, in addition to organizing supporters. Political campaigns against Tammany were often violent and bloody. Tammany fought hard and often unfairly to stay in power. There was constant concern in the La Guardia camp about illegal ballots and harassment of La Guardia voters at the polls. At some of La Guardia's outdoor meetings, bricks were thrown from roofs at the speakers and crowd. On one occasion, a baby carriage was hurled from a tenement roof at a La Guardia gathering. False fire alarms also were used to disrupt meetings. La Guardia used the *Ghibboni* to fight back against these tactics. Among their other duties, the *Ghibboni* served as guards, pollwatchers, and strong-arm men, if needed. They watched the roofs, fire-alarm boxes, and voting places to make sure that La Guardia, his speakers, and his voters were not harassed or attacked and that his ballots were not voided.

Given his progressive record in Congress, his national reputation, and his effective campaign organization, it was surprising that La Guardia lost his 1932 bid for reelection to the House. He ran that year on both the Republican ticket and on that of the quickly formed and short-lived Liberal party. His opponent was Tammany-picked Alderman James Lanzetta, the second Italian-American the Democrats had put up against La Guardia. This election year had looked like a strong one for Fiorello. He had a progressive platform, had been a major spokesman against Hoover and for relief and reform during the depression, and had secured support from other reform-minded politicians, such as Tammany's Robert Wagner and from labor, Republicans, Progressives, Independents, and Democrats.

He lost for a variety of reasons. Overconfidence was one. Lanzetta and Tammany worked hard to win back this district and were ahead of La Guardia in establishing contacts with Puerto Ricans migrating into the neighborhood. Tammany was aggressive in organizing and controlling the vote of this new group, whereas La Guardia and his people were lax in responding to the ethnic succession going on in the district as the Jews began to move out. It also is possible that some younger Italian-Americans identified more with Lanzetta than with the older La Guardia, although certainly Marcantonio and the young *Ghibboni* should have responded to and dealt with this problem. La Guardia's alleged neglect of his constituents was another factor in his defeat. Lanzetta attacked La Guardia for not doing enough for East Harlem and for being too concerned with national affairs. Most particularly, he accused Fiorello of neglecting his constituents' day-to-day needs for legal advice, immigration aid, and various other services. The busy La Guardia could not always be personally available, as he had been in the past, to assist his constituents, who at times insisted that he had to be there in person to help them. Some previously loyal voters therefore pulled away from Fiorello. However, La Guardia's organization was extremely active and was usually very good at addressing neighborhood needs. Another factor was Tammany's tampering with the vote count. Violence on both sides also occurred. These points taken together, plus a big vote in the area for Franklin Delano Roosevelt on the Democratic line, produced La Guardia's loss by 1,220 votes (16,447 for Lanzetta and 15,227 for La Guardia).

"A Pint of Liquid Dynamite"

La Guardia was certainly not finished, not even in Congress. As he returned to Congress for the end of its session after his November defeat, Adolf A. Berle, Jr., one of Roosevelt's brain-trusters, contacted him. Berle had met La Guardia in the summer of 1932 and had been impressed with him. He had spoken to Roosevelt about Fiorello and both had felt that La Guardia was a New Deal ally. After Roosevelt's election, La Guardia, a Republican, was asked to serve as congressional spokesman on behalf of the newly elected Roosevelt administration, to be the voice of the New Deal in Congress, and to propose its legislative program before Roosevelt took office in March. That in itself was affirmation of La Guardia's progressivism, his importance as a congressman and spokesman for reform, and his link between the reform of an earlier era and the New Deal reform of the depression period. La Guardia as a congressman had already proposed legislation that would evolve into New Deal programs; he had spoken for labor, farmers, and ethnics—the groups that made up the New Deal coalition—and he had supported Roosevelt's efforts as New York governor to counteract the depression. Fiorello also had the same vision as the New Dealers: that an activist government's new programs, its attempts to uplift the downtrodden (especially the unemployed) in order to improve the economic well-being of all societal segments, and its economic planning and support for labor unions would be effective in alleviating the suffering caused by the depression and in spurring recovery. Not all progressives agreed. Some saw the New Deal as an aberration, a program that passed because of an economic emergency and went beyond what had been advocated earlier. La Guardia, like Wagner, was a progressive who saw a link between the Progressive and New Deal reform movements. He had fought for a responsive government, social reform legislation and unions for years. La Guardia came to accept all aspects of the New Deal, even its deficit spending, to which he had first been opposed (as had Franklin Roosevelt).

Fiorello was active and effective as the voice of the New Deal. Berle, impressed with La Guardia, later referred to him as "a pint of liquid dynamite." This Congress passed the Twenty-first Amendment, which repealed Prohibition (the Eighteenth Amendment), and sent it to the states for ratification. It also passed amendments to the Federal Bankruptcy Act that offered some help to debtors through credit extensions and put the Interstate Commerce Commission rather than bankers in charge of bankrupt railroads' reorganization. La Guardia, while leading the support for this legislation, also spoke in favor of a farm relief plan, which presaged the Agricultural Adjustment Act of May 1933. He also led the fight to set up a Farm and Home Credit Bank, which would refinance mortgages at low interest rates (this was later passed under the Roosevelt administration in slightly different form). La Guardia was the spokesman in this Congress, as he had been many times before, for small businessmen, debtors, farmers, the poor, homeowners and others who needed help and protection.

La Guardia would bring this same thinking to his mayoral years and would once again link the Progressive and New Deal reform eras, speak for both an old and a new generation of reformers, and acknowledge the goals of the new ethnics.

CHAPTER FOUR

La Guardia as Mayor: The First Term

During his congressional career, La Guardia had linked different reform generations and different ethnic groups, speaking for the values and goals of an earlier generation of progressives as well as for those involved in the New Deal and reaching across ethnic boundaries. Nowhere is this role better revealed than in his mayoral years, during which Fiorello finally achieved a position that gave him the power and recognition he craved.

The Timing Was Not Right

La Guardia's first try for the mayoralty was, as noted earlier, his disastrous attempt in 1921 to secure the Republican nomination. He had also been urged to run for mayor in 1925 by some of his Progressive party supporters, but turned down the offer: that year was not a winnable one, Fiorello surmised. In 1929 he was willing to make the race again, this time with more backing. Because he was a good vote-getter and a leader of the Italian community, he was supported by Sam Koenig, the Republican boss, and by various Italian-American Republican organizations, and by those in the party who considered him a possible victor. Yet opposition also existed to his candidacy from Republicans who felt uncomfortable with an independent-minded politician who often attacked the policies and standard-bearers of his own party. Using tactics that had been successful before, La Guardia threatened that if he did not get the nomination he would take to the stump in the 1930 gubernatorial campaign and tell Republican voters how the party had declined to nominate him, a proven Tammany basher. This would embarrass the party and possibly help defeat the Republican nominee for governor. These were harsh tactics, but La Guardia was more loyal to principles than to parties, was intensely ambitious for high office, and believed he needed to win the mayor's position to continue helping the lower classes.

He secured the nomination, but many Republicans had little enthusiasm for his candidacy. Although La Guardia said he was a fusion candidate, independent Democrats kept their distance. As usual, La Guardia campaigned tirelessly and raised issues that were pertinent to the city's problems. He attacked Tammany's corruption and mismanagement of the city, spoke in favor of unifying New York's subway systems, dealt with such concerns as low-cost housing and building more parks and playgrounds, and advocated making the city government more efficient by streamlining the departmental structure. Most notably, he accused Tammany of having ties to New York gangsters.

At issue was the murder of Arnold Rothstein, a notorious gambler, bootlegger, and loan shark, who had been killed in November 1928. The police had been unable (or unwilling) to find the murderer. La Guardia stated that this inability was caused by Tammany's concern that an investigation would show the connections between politicians and criminals; therefore, the inquiry had been terminated. Jimmy Walker, who had been elected mayor in 1925, was La Guardia's Democratic opponent in 1929. The issue therefore could have severely damaged Walker's reelection bid. La Guardia had some evidence, and revealed a check from Rothstein to Magistrate Albert H. Vitale, indicating that the judge had borrowed $20,000 from the gambler. The money, which never was repaid, seemed to some to have been a bribe rather than a loan. Fiorello's charges of corruption in city government became important later as investigations proved him correct, but in 1929 the public, enjoying 1920s prosperity and Walker's wit, was not interested, and the issue fizzled.

Fiorello had difficulty securing the support of what should have been natural anti-Tammany allies—the good-government groups in the city. They did not as yet see La Guardia as a kindred spirit; instead, they saw him (erroneously) as only a power-hungry opportunist. There was a problem also in appealing to liberal elements, some of whom preferred the Socialist leader and mayoral candidate, Norman Thomas. Also running, as an independent, was former mayor John F. Hylan. He subsequently dropped out of the race and was replaced by Richard E. Enright, Hylan's police commissioner, who ran on a Square Deal ticket. However, even if La Guardia had run with Socialist and solid Republican and fusion support, he most likely would not have beaten Walker. Most of the campaign took place before the stock market crash at the end of October 1929. Awareness of a depression was not instantly evident and the public, for the most part, was still caught up in the spirit of 1920s prosperity. As Thomas Kessner writes in his biography of La Guardia, "The campaign pitted La Guardia's New York, foreign-speaking, economically depressed, a community seeking change and reform, against Walker's glittering capital of good times and easy living." Walker, a carefree, playboy mayor, symbolized the good times of the Jazz Age, of a fairy-tale New York, and his faults as a mayor, which were many, were overlooked.

The timing was not right for a progressive, independent-minded Italian-American Republican to win. It would take the shock of a depression, an awareness that the good times were really over, an awakening to Tammany's corruption, and an increased sense of the need for ethnic recognition among all Italian-Americans, even Tammany ones, to change the situation. In 1929, New York's largest Italian-American newspaper, the pro-Tammany *Il Progresso Italo-Americano*, declared for Walker. (Four years later, however, the paper took a strictly pro-Italian stand, endorsing all Italian-American candidates.) As a result of conditions in 1929, Fiorello lost in a Walker sweep of the city. Walker's vote was 867,522 to La Guardia's 367,675, the worst loss of any Republican-fusion mayoral candidate since the consolidation of the city in 1898. La Guardia, disappointed, went back to being a congressman, won reelection in 1930, and, as already noted, lost in 1932.

"Kind of a Magic Box?": The Tammany Scandals

Tammany's style of governing through favors and payoffs was ignored during the boom times of the 1920s. However, in a worsening economy, it no longer was acceptable to have grafting politicians mismanaging the public's money. The depression hit New York hard. The city's bustling, fast-paced economic activity slowed as the stock market crash and its aftermath created turmoil not only on Wall Street but also throughout New York's streets and boroughs. Thousands of people appeared on street corners trying to eke out a living selling apples at five cents apiece. Skilled workers and white-collar businessmen pounded the pavements looking for jobs. Families lost their livelihoods and, as evictions mounted, often their homes. Hospitals reported numerous cases of starvation. New York's bright lights and glitter were replaced by the grime of an impoverished city. In neighborhoods such as East Harlem and central Harlem (with its burgeoning black population that had migrated from the South), which had never benefited from 1920s prosperity, conditions were particularly dismal. Hoovervilles (shantytowns built by the urban poor on vacant land) and breadlines emerged, tensions increased, hope faded, and the people, looking desperately for leadership, cast a careful and disapproving eye at Tammany's antics. The first Tammany casualty of the depression was Magistrate Vitale. La Guardia's charge against Vitale during the 1929 campaign was valid; he did indeed have ties to gangsters and thus was removed from office in 1930 by the appellate division of the New York State Supreme Court.

Other investigations of Tammany-appointed judges led to new disclosures. Magistrate George F. Ewald, who had replaced Vitale, was suspected of selling worthless stock and was accused of purchasing his magistrate's job. Although Ewaid was never convicted, the charges against him, as well as various accusations against other judges, finally convinced Governor Franklin D. Roosevelt to take action. In August 1930 he called on the appellate division (which had jurisdiction over the lower courts) to begin a more extensive investigation of the magistrates' courts in Manhattan and the Bronx. The division complied and picked Samuel Seabury as the referee in the investigation that was begun with special council Isidore J. Kresel and a hard-working staff of young lawyers.

Seabury was a fortunate choice, not only because of his background, but also because of what he would contribute to La Guardia's career later. Born in 1873, he was part of that generation of socially prominent individuals who became active in politics in order to clean it up and bring in office holders from the better classes. Disgusted with corruption, political payoffs, and corporate influence in politics, Seabury was involved with the good-government forces who wished to bring honesty back to public service. He shared the same social class and thought process as Theodore Roosevelt. Seabury was the individual member of La Guardia's entourage of supporters who most clearly personified nineteenth-century political morality. He was in tune with Fiorello's thinking on honesty and efficiency in public office, and like La Guardia, but unlike many other patrician good-government types, also supported social reform. As a youth he had been influenced by single-tax advocate and early critic of monopolies Henry George. Later Seabury had supported William Jennings Bryan, Woodrow Wilson, and fusion reform mayors Seth Low and John Purroy Mitchel. Beyond his political attachments, he was a lawyer and had won office to the city court, state supreme court, and eventually to the highest court in the state, the state court of appeals. A reform Democrat who also received support from progressives of other parties during his political career, he had run for and lost the governorship in 1916. An anti-Tammany, good-government social reformer from Mayflower stock and the New York elite, Seabury eventually forged a logical but nonetheless unusual alliance with the Italian-American congressman representing East Harlem's slums.

Seabury's investigation of the magistrates' courts revealed extensive corruption and led to questions about corruption or misconduct in other branches of the city government. Governor Roosevelt in March 1931 appointed Seabury to investigate Manhattan District Attorney Thomas C. T. Crain. Again a picture of mismanagement and possible corruption emerged. At the very least, Crain had not been doing his job in dealing with various politically connected rackets. While Seabury was involved in these two investigations he was asked in April 1931 to serve as counsel for the Joint Legislative Committee to Investigate the Affairs of the City of New York, led by state Senator Samuel Hofstadter, in its study of corruption in the city. Seabury led three simultaneous investigations and was the individual people associated with the ferreting out of political corruption in the city. Although he did not have the authority to send anyone to prison, he could hold hearings and uncover wrongdoing.

The investigations revealed a sordid story of ties between politicians and criminals, payoffs, incompetence, and particularly the accumulation of large amounts of money by office holders with relatively modest salaries. One case was that of Thomas M. Farley, Tammany leader of the Fourteenth Assembly District and sheriff of New York county. With an annual salary of $8,500, Farley had been able to deposit in a bank almost $400,000 in six years. To Seabury's question as to how he had secured such wealth, Farley responded: "It represented moneys I had saved. I took the money out of a safe-deposit box at home." After further questioning, during which Farley discussed where the box was kept, the size of the box and safe, and what type of box it was (a tin box), Seabury asked where the money he had accumulated above his salary came from. Farley answered that it "came from the good box I had." "Kind of a magic box?" asked Seabury. "It was a wonderful box," responded Farley. Seabury retorted, "A wonderful box. What did you have to do—rub the lock with a little gold, and open it in order to find more money?" Farley's responses were the highlight of the hearings for the public, and Tin Box Parade now was the synonym for Seabury's investigations.

There were many other revelations. For example, Democratic office holders had taken $10,000 from the city's relief fund for 1931 to use for campaign purposes; this occurred during the depression, when poor people desperately needed relief money. The selling of franchises, permits, and political positions was widespread. The worst corruption was in the courts, however. Seabury revealed a situation in which bail bondsmen, police, an assistant district attorney, court officials, and lawyers had worked together in the women's court to extort money from prostitutes and to arrest innocent women and falsely charge them with prostitution in an effort to get them to pay fines or bail. These disclosures resulted in twenty-six individuals being forced out of the court system, the police ranks, and the office of the district attorney; six subsequently went to jail.

Eventually, the investigations and seemingly endless reports of corruption reached up to Mayor Walker, and he was called to testify in May 1932. Walker was questioned on payoffs to him, in the form of letters of credit, from businessmen who had dealings with the city. Most particularly, he was asked about a scheme to provide an exclusive bus franchise in New York to the Equitable Coach Company. Walker had secured the franchise for this bus company which, as it turned out, had no buses. Equitable was controlled by various businessmen, including some who were New York politicians. Also, J. A. Sisto had given Walker bonds worth $26,000. Sisto was involved in New York's taxicab business, and the bonds seemed to have bought political favors for the company in which Sisto had invested heavily. Some of these bonds were for a company that later secured a contract to make traffic-light posts for the city. Walker also had a secret account in a brokerage company, maintained by his financial agent, Russell T. Sherwood, that contained about $1 million. Walker tried to use ridicule, jokes, and alleged memory lapses to extricate himself. He also stated that some money came from gifts, not bribes, although the distinction between the two for a politician was tenuous. The case against Walker could not be absolutely proved, but it did lead to hearings before Governor Roosevelt to explain his activities. At the very least, Walker had to account convincingly for the discrepancy between his salary and the large amount of money he had accumulated. He could not, just as earlier Farley could not. As a result, rather than face dismissal by Roosevelt as Farley had, or embarrass the party, Walker decided to resign in September 1932, in the midst of the 1932 presidential campaign.

A City in Trouble

By this time Walker had severely hurt the city. Corruption was rife and bankruptcy was imminent. By 1931 the city was on the brink of economic collapse because of mismanagement combined with decreasing tax revenue and increasing relief requirements. This was not surprising, given a corrupt system that for example, maintained on the payroll city workers who had died years earlier. Budgets served the needs of the machine, not the city. New York had suffered through years of neglect under Walker. He had allowed the physical infrastructure of the city to deteriorate, problems to go unsolved, and corruption to run rampant. The depression accentuated all these faults. The mayor, who had governed poorly in good times, could not cope with the demands of the difficult depression era.

As New York teetered on the edge of bankruptcy, Walker was forced to approach the banks for help in early 1932. The banks agreed to save New York, but only in return for supervision of its economy. The bankers pressured the city into a policy of retrenchment, urging city leaders to cut back on projects, jobs, and salaries in order to balance the budget. Through 1932, as the baton of city power passed from Walker to others, New York's economic health did not improve amidst squabbling over job, salary, and other budget reductions.

After Walker's resignation, Joseph V. McKee, president of the Board of Aldermen and tied to the Bronx machine of Edward J. Flynn, served as acting mayor until a special election could be held in November to pick someone to serve out the one year left in Walker's term. McKee did a creditable job, but Tammany chose surrogate court judge

and stalwart Tammany man John P. O'Brien as the Democratic mayoral nominee. He won against Republican Lewis
H. Pounds (a former Brooklyn borough president), Socialist Morris Hillquit, and a substantial write-in vote for
McKee (11.8 percent of the vote), which appeared to be a
good-government vote. Clearly, Tammany was still in control. The machine did not suddenly collapse as a result of
the Seabury investigations. However, with a deepening of
the depression, the emergence of a strong fusion candidate
who could appeal to the city's ethnic groups, and a hostile
Democratic administration in Washington, Tammany's days
of unchecked power were limited.

O'Brien proved to be an ineffective mayor for a city in
economic decline. His failure was in part because of his
poor relations with Roosevelt. The president was angry at
Tammany for its lack of support for his nomination in 1932
and gave his blessing to the Bronx and Brooklyn Democratic machines of Edward J. Flynn and Frank Kelly, respectively (Kelly became Brooklyn boss in 1934). As a result
of the coolness between O'Brien and Roosevelt, New York's
economic problems did not receive the federal attention required to deal with them. There was no easy flow of information or effective cooperation between New York and
Washington. A further source of friction between the
mayor and the president was that O'Brien, like Walker before him, allowed Tammany to gain control of, and subsequently mismanage, the relief structure in New York. The
city economy was clearly hurt, therefore, not only by the
distant relationship between the local and national leadership, but also by Tammany chicanery. However, even more
detrimental than these factors to New York's economic recovery was Mayor O'Brien's attitude toward federal help.
O'Brien did not like the idea of federal loans and was reluctant to urge the federal government to provide more
aid. He preferred to secure loans from banks to fund the
relief system and save the city. He also was slow in making

use of federal funds, as for example from the Public Works Administration (PWA), which had already been appropriated in June 1933. In the summer of 1933 federal officials stated that future aid would be provided only to those local and state governments that had balanced budgets.

At the behest of the banks and in an effort to please federal officials and avoid bankruptcy, O'Brien did make an effort to balance the city budget. He also tried to streamline the municipal government as well as cut costs by abolishing certain positions, restructuring departments, and lowering salaries, including his own. A fall 1933 bankers agreement with O'Brien requested that in return for more loans to run New York, covering the period to 1937, the city had to curtail real estate tax increases and maintain a reserve to pay off the bank loans in case of slow or delinquent tax payments to the city (tax money was used to pay the banks). Also, a tax on the utility companies was imposed and bonds were issued to generate income for the relief system. In this way, the banks would have first access to all other tax monies and not be accused of taking funds away from the needy. O'Brien's agreements and programs avoided immediate bankruptcy but never went far enough to solve the city's economic problems. Although the banks were willing to lend more money to the city in light of O'Brien's efforts, New York's credit rating declined and poverty grew worse. The relief problems and continued cases of corruption and mismanagement in city government under Tammany led to the fusion effort of 1933.

Fusion, 1933

The various anti-Tammany, reform, and Republican groups that could not merge in a fusion movement for the 1932 special election managed to do so in 1933. These groups included the newly formed (in 1932) City party which was called the City Fusion party in 1933 when it joined with the Republicans in a fusion effort. A number of candidates were proposed before La Guardia got the nomination in August 1933. Seabury, of course, was a logical choice, but he declined. So did McKee and Al Smith, as well as prominent social worker and reformer Raymond V. Ingersoll; Richard C. Patterson, Jr., a vice-president of NBC and corrections commissioner in the Walker years; John C. Knox, a United States district judge; Clarence J. Shearn, a former justice of the state supreme court; Nathan Straus, Jr., a civic leader and businessman; George V. McLaughlin, a banker and Walker administration police commissioner; and Peter Grimm, a well-known realtor. All, except perhaps Smith, were independent Democrats. They declined for various political and personal reasons, but the important question is why the fusion group did not immediately turn to La Guardia, a well-known reformer and independent Republican who clearly wanted the nomination.

The Fusion Conference Committee (which had been charged with finding a candidate) included a number of individuals who did not care for La Guardia. Made up of conservative Republicans, businessmen, and good-government people, the selection committee actually represented old-stock, upper-middle-class New Yorkers who tended to look down on the aggressive, flamboyant ethnic from East Harlem. La Guardia tried his old tactics to get the nomination, threatening to enter the Republican party primary as an independent and take that nomination. Without the Republicans, a fusion ticket stood little chance.

However, it was not threats but the support of some prominent individuals who knew La Guardia and were influential within good-government ranks that secured the nomination for him. Adolf Berle, Jr., the New Deal advisor who had worked with La Guardia during his last few months in Congress, backed Fiorello and spoke highly of his efforts to secure the passage of Roosevelt's legislation.

As Berle's biographer, Jordan A. Schwarz, relates, Berle believed in La Guardia's ability as "a street-wise 'gut-fighter'
who knew how to get honorable results" and who could be
effective against Tammany. Berle also brought La Guardia's
name to Seabury's attention in the spring of 1933 as a possibility for the fusion nomination. Although Seabury did
not declare for La Guardia, he now seriously considered
him. At least he became convinced that Fiorello was not
just an ambitious, uncouth, loud-mouthed politician. It was
La Guardia's style, not his politics, that appeared to bother
Seabury. Berle pointed out what a concerned reformer and
honest office holder La Guardia was. Berle at this point
also became part of a group that was associated with
Seabury and comprised such prominent reformers as
Charles C. Burlingham, a long-time good-government advocate whose voice carried much weight in reform circles
and who would form a close bond of friendship with Fiorello. This group also included former Bull Moose Progressives, New Freedom Democrats, and New Dealers, as well
as (and sometimes the same people) Republicans interested
in reforming their party. These individuals were to be the
driving force in La Guardia's selection as the nominee.
Berle set up a meeting between La Guardia and this group,
but Seabury, although more favorable to Fiorello, still
held back his endorsement. Meanwhile, Vito Marcantonio
whipped up Italian support and deluged Seabury with petitions supporting La Guardia's nomination.

Eventually, the selection came down to three individuals:
Robert Moses, secretary of state in Al Smith's gubernatorial
administration and the man responsible for developing the
park system in New York state; General John P. O'Ryan,
who had been the commander of the Twenty-seventh Division during the war, and was in 1933 a lawyer and one of
the leaders of the new City Fusion party; and La Guardia.

Moses was the Fusion Conference Committee's first
choice, but Seabury refused to support him because of Mo-

ses's ties with Al Smith (a reformer but still a Tammany man). Getting no help from Al Smith and opposed by Seabury, Moses pulled himself out of consideration in an effort to maintain unity in fusion ranks. By this time Seabury had decided to back La Guardia. The committee then offered the nomination to O'Ryan, and again Seabury protested. La Guardia continued to threaten throughout the discussions to enter the Republican primary or run as an independent if he did not get the nomination. After much discussion and maneuvering, which resulted in the formation of a new "harmony" nominating committee, chaired by Burlingham and comprising some of the Seabury group (Republican state chairman W. Kingsland Macy and Berle), most of the Fusion Conference Committee, and others, Seabury was able to push through La Guardia's nomination. He ran on the Republican and City Fusion tickets.

Seabury stated to the press after the nomination that "the selection of Fiorello H. La Guardia to lead the Fusion ticket . . . presents to the voters . . . an opportunity to express their indignation and disgust with Tammany Hall and its methods by the election of an honest, fearless, and capable anti-Tammany mayor; a sincere and militant opponent of graft, corruption and waste, who will put an end to the squandering and wasting of the people's money by Tammany Hall for the enrichment of the politicians and their friends and restore it to unemployment relief, schools, hospitals and the other purposes for which it was intended." La Guardia issued his own statement, noting that this race was going to be more than a contest between politicians; it would be "a citizens movement for the salvation of the city."

Seabury and La Guardia represented the hostility to Tammany boss rule that came primarily from two elements—the older generation of old stock good-government activists and progressives and the younger generation of anti-Tammany newer ethnics—mainly Italians and

Jews. These groups were from different classes, lived in different worlds in New York, and represented different groups, but were linked by their support of La Guardia, who managed to speak for both. Much like the New Deal coalition, La Guardia represented and pulled together an eclectic following based on ethnic and reform factors. He stood for the values of nineteenth-century good-government advocates, twentieth-century progressives, and urban ethnics.

"Would You Say These Ideas Are Radical?" The 1933 Campaign

The 1933 election showed all these forces at work. La Guardia pitched his campaign at those who were dissatisfied with Tammany's corruption, mismanagement, or lack of ethnic representation. O'Brien ran for reelection on the Democratic ticket as Tammany's candidate. The first noticeable contrast between the fusion and Democratic efforts was in their choice of candidates for various offices. Fusion chose an ethnically balanced ticket, whereas Tammany went with the usual predominantly Irish candidates. An Italian-American was the mayoral hopeful, and Bernard Deutsch, previous head of the Bronx County Bar Association and president of the American Jewish Congress, was selected as the fusion candidate for president of the Board of Aldermen. An Irish leader, W. Arthur Cunningham, became the nominee for comptroller. Joseph A. Palma became the first Italian-American to be chosen as a candidate for borough president (he ran in Staten Island). Fusion, under La Guardia, was reaching out for the Italian and Jewish vote. Many Italians saw in La Guardia in 1933 a real possibility of an Italian mayor and supported him on that basis. As the *Sons of Italy Magazine* stated in 1933:

> For nearly a score of years a struggle has been carried on by those of our race in America for public recognition in the pop-

ulous centers in which live substantial numbers of Italo-Americans. . . . The tendency has . . . been for those of other racial origins who have preceded us in this country to retain the privileges they had taken for themselves, enlarge them, if possible, and exclude others as long as possible from a just portion of representation in the public offices. . . . In helping to elevate one of our race to an important public office, it must be remembered that we are helping ourselves and our individual aspirations for future realization because in almost each case the occupancy of a public office by an Italo-American establishes a precedent for that office which then receives permanent consideration.

Tammany virtually ignored the Italian vote but did include a Jewish nominee, Milton Solomon, for president of the Board of Aldermen.

La Guardia looked like a sure winner. O'Brien had not been a successful mayor during his one-year stewardship. Also, Tammany corruption and bossism were still important issues, and La Guardia made good use of these concerns. The fusion slate was not only ethnically balanced but also included a number of prominent reformers long associated with good-government forces in New York. Fiorello's rhetoric indicated his differences with Tammany. An example was his answer to accusations that he was dangerous and a radical: "I suppose I really am dangerous, but not dangerous to honest men, whether they be poor or rich. I have been dangerous to crooks, no matter how high their position. Perhaps I have been radical, too, in advocating policies which have been adopted several years after I proposed them and I have been radical in fighting against existing evils." He noted also that earlier in his political career he had "warned the city of the danger of bankruptcy. A city no more than an individual can borrow itself out of debt. City accounts should be public so that an average business man can see exactly what is happening. Would you say these ideas are radical?"

La Guardia's hope for an easy victory was dashed when Joseph V. McKee entered the contest, running on the Recovery party ticket. According to Edward Flynn, Democratic boss of the Bronx, Roosevelt was the inspiration for the Recovery party. He had asked Flynn to persuade McKee to make the race for mayor and said that he would publicly come out for McKee at the appropriate moment. Also, Jim Farley (a close Roosevelt advisor, his postmaster general, and chairman of the national and state Democratic party) had been asked to convince McKee to run. Roosevelt apparently was still angry at Tammany's lack of support for him at the Democratic convention in 1932 and wanted to gain command over the party in New York through Flynn's Bronx organization and McKee. Flynn, who had backed Roosevelt's nomination, had also disagreed with various Tammany decisions and stated that a split had already begun to form between the Bronx and Tammany (Manhattan) machines. Moreover, Roosevelt was also concerned that an enhanced Republican party under a fusion administration might detrimentally affect his reelection bid in 1936 and that of Governor Herbert Lehman in 1934. Bringing McKee into the contest could accomplish two goals: weakening Tammany and keeping a Republican out of the mayor's position. Both goals suited Roosevelt, Flynn, and Farley.

McKee was a formidable candidate and probably would have been the fusion choice had he kept himself in contention for that nomination. He could attract Republicans who were discontented with La Guardia's selection, as well as independent Democrats, New Deal supporters, and anti-Tammany individuals of both parties. However, the McKee candidacy also hurt O'Brien and split the Democratic organization in the city. Although the Recovery party also went after the new ethnic vote, and therefore offered more recognition to the new groups, it fell far short of the fusion effort in this regard. McKee, who was Irish, had as a run-

ning mate Nathan Straus, Jr., a prominent Jewish businessman, who was a candidate for president of the Board of
Aldermen. (All three parties ran Jewish candidates for this
post.) The Recovery party also included Ferdinand Pecora,
an Italian, as the nominee for Manhattan district attorney.
Fusion's ethnically balanced slate forced the other two parties in this direction, primarily in relation to the Jewish
vote. Italians received nominations in the two Democratic
parties, but only for lesser positions. In nominations for aldermen throughout the city, again it was the fusion ticket
that tried to appeal to the newer groups. For sixty-five aldermanic positions open in this election, the Democratic
nominees included twenty-five Irish, six Jews, five Germans, and three Italians. The rest could not be identified
ethnically. The Recovery party, running for only thirty-
four seats, chose twelve Irish, four Jews, three Germans,
and one Italian. The fusion slate was decidedly different
with fewer Irish candidates (six) and more Jews (fifteen)
and Italians (six). The fusion approach entailed easier access to positions and more recognition for Italians and
Jews.

La Guardia and McKee fought over who was the real
choice of the New Deal. Each declared himself to be the
real reform, anti-Tammany candidate. Fiorello accused
McKee of being a front man for Tammany and under Boss
Flynn's control. With Seabury often on the platform with
him, Fiorello proclaimed himself as the good-government
candidate supporting honesty and efficiency in government, a new city charter, a streamlined city bureaucracy, a
balanced budget, and a nonpartisan leadership. This strategy was effective, because the McKee ticket, which was less
balanced ethnically than the fusion slate, also was not as
balanced as to good-government reformers. La Guardia
had a monopoly of those associated with Seabury and with
the City Fusion party (who with the Republicans made up
the joint fusion slate). One difference between the two can-

didates was noted by Ogden Mills, a Republican politician, who commented that McKee's plan was to reform Tammany from the inside, whereas La Guardia believed the only way to change it was to smash it from the outside. The more important issue was which party contained the New Dealers. Both could claim New Deal advisors and supporters. La Guardia had Berle, but McKee was backed by Farley and Raymond Moley (a New Deal brain-truster).

Flynn waited for Roosevelt's promised endorsement of McKee (although Farley claimed that all Roosevelt had agreed to do was publicly invite McKee to the White House). Roosevelt said nothing. Berle was apparently influential in getting Roosevelt to stay neutral; he spoke to Roosevelt about La Guardia's attributes for the mayor's position and the need for the president to stay out of New York's politics. Although McKee continued to portray himself as the New Deal candidate, Roosevelt's failure to endorse him considerably weakened that image and thereby helped La Guardia.

La Guardia attacked O'Brien for not reaching out for more federal relief funds. Fiorello, noting his own long-standing concern for the poor, stated that he would be more effective in this area. La Guardia promised that his vision of a caring government, which included a relief system free of political influence, more jobs for the unemployed, a better city health-care system, more parks and recreational areas, better housing, and fewer slums would be fulfilled. La Guardia forged a link between good-government advocates and the disadvantaged by stating that honest and efficient government would have as its goal help for the poor and the improvement of their environment. La Guardia set out a concept of government and life in New York beyond what "reformer" McKee suggested.

Although there was much talk about reform and bossism, ethnic issues generated the most heat in the campaign and possibly cost McKee the election. Ethnic-oriented campaigns were normal fare in multicultural New York, and it was an easy tactic for politicians to appeal to ethnic loyalties and emotions. However, this was also a dangerous tactic that could easily split the city as well as backfire on the vote-seeker. As noted already, the fusion ticket appealed more strongly to the new ethnic voter, as reflected in its ethnically balanced slate of candidates. Each mayoral candidate nonetheless tried to secure the endorsements of prominent ethnic leaders and organizations. The support of the various German-American newspapers and clubs was split between the three candidates. The Irish-American press and societies in the city endorsed the two Irish candidates, O'Brien and McKee, with the Democratic candidate getting more support. La Guardia did get some Irish backing (an Irish-American League for Fusion was set up) but most Irish voters supported the Irish-controlled Tammany and Flynn machines. Italian-Americans were strongly behind their fellow ethnic.

The large Jewish vote was unpredictable. All the candidates secured newspaper and organizational support. La Guardia, who had received many Jewish votes in his earlier congressional contests, spoke Yiddish and was involved in issues of interest to the Jewish community. However, he was not seen yet as the one local politician who could respond most strongly to the 1930s fears and hopes of this group in regard to political positions and the Nazi terror; that recognition would come later in the 1930s. The Jewish community therefore became the battleground of the campaign as each candidate sought the Jewish vote.

McKee's team made the initial pitch to Jewish voters. They suggested that Seabury's speeches, which criticized Governor Herbert Lehman for not taking legal action against a few corrupt Tammany district leaders, were anti-Semitic. Although no anti-Semitism was evident in Seabury's statements, this allegation could have weakened La Guardia in the Jewish community, where Lehman was a highly respected figure. However, McKee soon found out what Fiorello's opponent in 1922, Henry Frank, had realized too late—that Fiorello was extremely skillful at using ethnic issues to win an election.

La Guardia introduced into the campaign a *Catholic World* essay that McKee had written in 1915 as proof of McKee's anti-Semitism. According to Paul Windels, who had been campaign manager during Fiorello's race for president of the Board of Aldermen in 1919 and one of his campaign managers in the 1933 contest, La Guardia had been well aware of McKee's article but was not going to use it in the campaign. However, he changed his mind after McKee introduced the issue of anti-Semitism into the contest. Ernest Cuneo commented that "Fiorello [in an earlier election] said he always deplored the spurious racial issue [in campaigns], but if that was the game the guy wanted to play, that was the game he was going to get." McKee was aware of the damaging possibilities of his earlier writings and had already removed copies of the article from all of the city libraries. La Guardia's people finally found a copy in the congressional library in Washington.

The article was difficult for McKee to explain, and La Guardia, of course, called for an explanation. In the essay, McKee had appealed to Catholic parents to be certain that their children attended high school. Contrasting Catholics with Jews, who did make sure their children went to school and therefore made up a large majority of the city's high school population, he noted that the Jews therefore would become the leaders, "the professional men of the coming generation." McKee proclaimed that these Jews were abandoning the moral tenets of Judaism in their striving for material advancement. "Surely," he noted, "we cannot look for ideal results from such material." McKee pictured Jewish students as morally corrupt and noted that Catholic youths, because of their lack of education, would be subservient to the Jews in the future. McKee warned Catholics not to let this happen.

McKee made a last-ditch effort to defuse the issue by going on radio and stating that he had meant to condemn only those Jews who had turned away from their religion, not all Jews. There is no question that the issue hurt McKee. He lost some Jewish support, even among his prominent backers, and faced continued attacks from La Guardia on this issue. In 1933, with Hitler and Nazism assuming power in Germany, charges of anti-Semitism had particular importance. Many Jewish New Yorkers, however, did not believe the accusations against McKee and gave him continued support because of his previous good relations with the Jewish community. Others simply were disgusted with the introduction of an ethnic-religious issue into a contest that supposedly was concentrating on Tammany abuses. Nonetheless, McKee had played into La Guardia's hands and had allowed Fiorello to emerge as a defender of the Jews. In this case, ethnic appeals served as an effective way to beat the Democratic machines at their own game.

How successful were the ethnic tactics? La Guardia won the election with 40.4 percent of the vote to McKee's 28.3 percent and O'Brien's 27.2 percent. This victory came just one year after Roosevelt, running as a Democrat, had swept the city with a 66.4 percent vote. The ethnic group that went the most strongly for La Guardia was the Italians, who gave him 62.2 percent of the vote within Italian election districts, with 23.7 percent for O'Brien and 11.3 percent for McKee. The Jewish election districts gave La Guardia a 36.3 percent vote, with 31.9 percent for O'Brien and 22.7 percent for McKee. His plurality here was based on the split in the Democratic organization caused by McKee, the attraction of good-government reform and Republicanism, especially to upper- and middle-class Jewish voters, and the issue of anti-Semitism. La Guardia received his lowest votes from New York's Irish, securing only 21.8 percent of their vote, with 36.9 percent going to O'Brien and 39.5 percent to McKee. Many Irish apparently decided to stay with the Irish-controlled machines rather than support an Italian Republican who threatened to usurp Irish political control of the city for Italians and Jews. The vote in the German election districts was 30 percent for Fiorello, 45.4 percent for McKee, and 22.5 percent for O'Brien. The black vote has never been systematically analyzed, but if the vote in the predominantly black Twenty-first Assembly District in Harlem can be used as a guide to the preferences of the city's black voters, La Guardia did well, securing 39.6 percent of the vote in this district. The La Guardia victory, then, was largely the product of the Italian vote across all income classes, upper- and middle-class Jewish votes, and apparently the black vote as well.

Ethnic Succession in "This Most Irish of Cities"

Even before La Guardia identified himself as a progressive, he had seen himself as a spokesman for the immigrants who arrived in New York City in the late nineteenth and early twentieth centuries. From his youth in Arizona through his consular and Ellis Island experiences and into his political career, Fiorello identified with the Italians and Jews who came to America. Their aspirations, grievances, and desire for recognition and acceptance reflected his own. As a fighter for the dispossessed and powerless, La Guardia spoke for blacks as well. And the emerging white ethnics and blacks needed to have a powerful voice speaking for them and against the persistent nativism and racism of America. As protector, spokesman, and symbol, La Guardia changed the ethnic power hierarchy in the city and considerably diminished Irish political control. The ethnic aspects of the 1933 election represented the beginnings of that change.

La Guardia's 1933 victory was met with an outburst of celebration in the Italian community. In Greenwich Village, the densely packed slums of East Harlem, the tenements of the East Bronx, and the small one- and two-family homes of Brooklyn's Canarsie and Queens' Corona, Italian New York erupted in celebration. The usually pro-Tammany *Il Progresso* best expressed the Italian reaction: "Only a few years back we were in last place; today the Italians are able to decide the outcome of a great contest and bring Fiorello La Guardia to one of the highest and most valued public offices of this country."

Some ethnic groups reacted with less enthusiasm, seeing in La Guardia a change that they neither expected nor desired. The Irish newspaper *Gaelic American*, for example, commented unhappily about the success of an Italian mayoral candidate over an Irish one in "this most Irish of cities." Some of the Irish viewed La Guardia's ascent to the mayoralty as the beginning of the end of Irish political hegemony in New York.

Both ethnic groups were somewhat correct; La Guardia's victory did represent a decided change, and he would work to bring about even more changes; however, the rise of Italian power and the decline of the Irish was not as precipitous or total as the Italians hoped and the Irish feared. Yet, a shift from past practices was evident. For example, in the early period of Mayor Walker's administration, the eight-member Board of Estimate included five Irish, one German, and one Jew (those who could be identified ethnically). In 1934, during the La Guardia administration, there were three Irish, two Jews, and two Italians (identified ethnically out of eight board members). Generally more Jews and Italians served in the La Guardia administrations than under Tammany mayors. An analysis of mayoral cabinet appointments done by political scientist

Theodore Lowi revealed that Walker's and O'Brien's cabinet appointees were about 25 percent and 41 percent Irish, respectively; under La Guardia the Irish dropped to 5 percent of appointees. The Jews went from about 9 percent (Walker) to 7 percent (O'Brien) to 15 percent (La Guardia), and the Italians saw an increase from 1 percent (Walker) to 3 percent (O'Brien) to about 5 percent (La Guardia).

Fiorello was particularly interested in appealing to the Jewish vote, which he needed to win future elections. The Italians presumably were already in his camp, as they gave him a resounding majority of their vote in 1933. As such Fiorello did not have to win them over as much and this attitude is reflected in his upper level appointments. For example, by his second term, there were six Jews and only one Italian who could be identified out of his nineteen department commissioners. However, Italians made their gains too, moving into lower-level city government and various court positions appointed by the mayor. Considering just the magistrates' courts, by 1944 there were seven Italian city magistrates, compared to only one in this position under Tammany in 1925. Notable also was the number of blacks chosen for city office. La Guardia appointed the first black judge in New York, Myles A. Paige of the court of special sessions, and the first black female judge in the United States, Jane M. Bolin of the domestic relations court. He also promoted a black fireman, Captain Wesley Williams, to be the first black battalion chief in the department, and appointed Samuel A. Battle in 1941 as the first black on the parole board. As Jewish, Italian, and black representation increased in various levels of city government, the Irish presence decreased.

La Guardia's election also brought a shift in ethnic access to civil service appointments. Under Tammany, Jews, Italians, and blacks had difficulty getting civil service jobs, which went mostly to the Irish. La Guardia increased the number of civil service jobs in the competitive category, meaning that applicants had to take exams that determined their place on the list for a position. In 1933, when he became mayor, 54.5 percent of the city workers were in the competitive class; by 1939, 74.3 percent were in this group. The number of exempt (appointive) and noncompetitive jobs were reduced. He thereby removed much of the political influence involved in securing civil service positions. By supporting an antidiscrimination policy in city employment, La Guardia opened up these jobs to all. In addition, he tried to end graft and discrimination in the promotion system for city workers. Using exams and rankings, city employees could now win promotions based on merit and without political connections. La Guardia's new policies increased the number of blacks in the civil service and provided better jobs for those already working for the city. Blacks now were able to become conductors, dispatchers, and motormen on the subways, whereas before they could be only porters. Between 1934 and 1941, forty-six blacks were appointed firemen; in the period from 1898 to 1934, only three had secured this position. The same was true for other city departments: from 1898 to 1934, only four blacks were appointed in the Department of Corrections as compared to twenty-eight under La Guardia from 1934 to 1941. Among the professional civil service category (doctors, dentists, supervisors), the number of blacks went from 79 before 1934 to 265 from 1934 to 1941.

In political positions, such as elective offices, where the mayor's power could not be used in quite the same way, the Democratic party under Irish control still held sway. But there were changes even here as the Democratic machines responded to Jewish and Italian pressure and to La Guardia's ethnic appeal. As earlier, the Democrats were more interested in the better organized and more variable Jewish vote, but became more open to Italian representation as they tried to win this vote. For example, on the state level, Charles Poletti became lieutenant governor in 1938, joining the Jewish Governor, Herbert Lehman, who had served since 1932. Peter Brancato, at the suggestion of Frank Kelly, Democratic boss of Brooklyn, became the first Italian county judge in 1935. And in 1936 Matthew Abruzzo, again with Kelly's support, was appointed by the president as the first federal judge of Italian background. Among the city's state senate seats and in the New York City congressional delegation, there were more Jews than Italians, but the Irish maintained control over these positions.

La Guardia was able to use his Italian appointments in particular to political advantage, and this forced the Democrats to acknowledge this group as well. In 1937 the mayor's Italian Re-election Committee stated that "In New York City, the biggest Italian city in the world, we have with the Fusion administration begun to achieve the first genuine measure of representation in government. . . . A new day has arrived!" The Irish Democrats were put on the defensive and had to respond. Although they were aware of how eagerly the Italian community sought recognition, they did not really wish to share power. They hoped that the Italians could be satisfied with a minimal number of positions while the Irish retained control of the party. Although the Italians received some high-level appointments, ethnic control of the real power of the party, the patronage-laden district leaderships, shifted very slowly and, at times, not by choice. Yet, the Irish leadership could see that change was inevitable, as evidenced not only by La Guardia's Italian vote, but also in the pages of such publications as *Il Progresso*, which in 1934 expressed the Italian community's desire for more political recognition and saw the group's political emergence as only beginning.

La Guardia's terms in office not only signified to the Irish the necessity of recognizing other groups, but also a decline in their own political power and status. The mayor, who had wooed Irish voters earlier in his career, seemed determined to do nothing that would indicate that this group (so identified with Tammany) still had a voice at City Hall. An incident early in his first administration reveals Fiorello's attitude toward the Irish.

In 1934, La Guardia chose Dr. Charles Fama, an Italian Protestant, to be the medical examiner for New York's Employee's Retirement System. The choice of Fama was controversial because of charges that he had written anti-Catholic articles and had been critical of Irish Catholic political power in the city. Irish organizations and newspapers protested that Fama's anti-Irish and anti-Catholic statements should disqualify him for the city job. The mayor was not sympathetic to Irish demands and kept Fama on the job. His rationale was that the doctor was qualified for the position and that was the only criterion. The anger in the Irish community was reflected in its press. As the *Gaelic American* stated, "It is very evident that our Mayor has little regard for the opinions of people of Irish blood." Usually, La Guardia was immediately responsive to charges of bigotry and would work to eliminate the problem. That he did not in this case suggests an insensitivity to Irish Catholic concerns based, perhaps, on his lack of desire to acknowledge a group that Italians and Jews saw as their main opponents in New York's political battles. This incident, combined with the decline of Irish appointees under La Guardia, seems to form a pattern. The Irish community continued to feel throughout the decade that the mayor was not responsive to their needs. Fiorello was too smart a politician not to understand what he was doing and why New York's Irish could resent his actions. However, as Jews and Italians asserted themselves and gained more power during the 1930s, La Guardia clearly put himself at the forefront of their political succession, helping it along, claiming it as his own, and using it to win elections. Pleasing the Irish was a liability in a political world in which Jews and Italians saw the Irish as already having too much control. Although Irish political power never declined as much as the Irish thought (they actually retained much power and would eventually retake the mayoralty), their perceptions of decline as other groups challenged their hegemony were strong.

A Different Sort of Mayor: "Where's the Wastebasket!"

La Guardia offered a new approach in managing the mayor's office. During the campaign and again upon winning, he told his Republican district leaders and campaign workers not to expect positions in his administration unless they were capable of doing the job. "My first qualification for this great office," he noted, "is my monumental personal ingratitude. I want you to remember that a cause, not a man, has succeeded. . . . I will hire the best men for every job, even if they happened to vote against me." Later Fiorello was to insist that his commissioners and other top appointees resign from all political party positions, an action that would not endear him to those Republicans and City Fusion party members who had worked for him and expected rewards while maintaining their party power. This policy weakened the new City Fusion party in the long run as it lost the talents of leaders who took administrative posts.

La Guardia was sworn in as mayor in Seabury's house in the early morning hours of January 1, 1934. He said after the ceremony that "our theory of municipal government is an experiment, to try to show that a nonpartisan, nonpolitical local government is possible, and, if we succeed, I am sure success in other cities is possible." Fiorello was at work early on New Year's Day, diving into the mess left behind by the previous administrations and showing an energy in office that New Yorkers were not used to seeing in their mayors. He literally attacked the mountain of letters waiting for him at the office, responding to them by telling his secretary to "say yes, . . . say no, . . . tell him to go to hell . . . ," and, most importantly, "Where's the wastebasket! . . . That's going to be the most important file around City Hall." The new mayor was no easy touch.

The job he faced was enormous. He had to deal with an economically depressed city with large numbers of unemployed, a poor credit rating, a political system rife with corruption and mismanagement after years of Tammany control, and public works programs at a standstill. Also, the Democratic machines (mainly Tammany and the Bronx machine) were still very strong. Even after the La Guardia victory in 1933, they held on to the Board of Aldermen, the borough presidencies of the Bronx and Manhattan, the district attorney's position in Manhattan, and numerous lesser offices, and continued to show strength in the years to come. La Guardia had to prove that good government could deal with the depression. He also had to weaken the Democratic machine control of the city, and eliminate as much corruption as possible in city departments. Fiorello tried to accomplish these tasks by bringing together the philosophies of good government inspired by municipal civic and social reformers of the nineteenth century and progressives of the early twentieth century with the concepts of the New Deal. He espoused an efficient, corruption-free, democratic government that was concerned with social justice and used the 1930s approaches of economic planning, aggressive government intervention in the economy, and a stronger welfare-state emphasis. "Government with a soul," Fiorello called it. La Guardia, like Franklin D. Roosevelt, looked backward and forward in his quest for a more responsive government. Both were optimistic believers in progress who bridged two reform movements and served as brokers between the various contending groups in society.

Fiorello's generally nonpartisan, good-government approach is evident in the appointments of his city department heads. Especially when compared to his predecessors at City Hall, La Guardia's appointments indicate a commitment to the merit system and to securing the best-qualified people no matter what party they belonged to or where they lived in the country. As the mayor noted, "there is no Democratic or Republican way of cleaning the streets." He looked for experts in various fields and usually brought very well qualified individuals into his government. For example, Robert Moses, who had been so successful developing the state's parks, was appointed commissioner of the parks department; William R. Hudson, a social worker and the executive director of the Welfare Council of New York City, became the commissioner of public welfare; William Fellowes Morgan, Jr., who had been involved in combatting the corruption at the Fulton Fish Market and was head of the National Fisheries Association, was appointed commissioner of markets. For fire commissioner, he chose John J. McElligott, the only fire commissioner of this period who had actually been a fireman. La Guardia even reached into the earlier Democratic administration and continued the tenure of Commissioner of Docks John McKenzie, who had been doing a good job in that position. Regardless of what the mayor said, however, even initially not all appointments were nonpolitical and based strictly on merit; ethnic and political considerations played some role. Frederick J. Kracke, Kings County Republican committee chairman, became commissioner of plants and structures. Adolf A. Berle, Jr., New Deal brain-truster, close La Guardia advisor, and fusion activist, was appointed city chamberlain (although this was a political appointment, Berle was qualified for the job). La Guardia's people were far more professional then those chosen by his predecessors, and politics played a much smaller role in his appointments.

Below the level of department head, the new mayor's civil service reforms were responsible for bringing better qualified individuals into government service. La Guardia diligently supervised the changes in the civil service, even personally going over the exams to determine whether they were fair.

La Guardia's intent was to rid the various departments of political hangers-on and, as he called them, "clubhouse loafers" and replace them with able people. For example, he told Austin McCormick, his Department of Corrections commissioner, to get rid of all the subordinates in this corrupt government group and begin anew with fresh people. Other department heads got the message and went to work. A good deal of the effort to eliminate corruption and waste was done by the Department of Investigations (initially called Department of Accounts), which looked into various charges and complaints and worked with the other departments to deal with numerous problems. For example, in the Department of Purchase, coal sellers and department personnel defrauded the city on the amount of coal delivered. At the city's home for the poor and elderly, Tammany supervisors cheated these unfortunate residents out of what little money they had. In Queens, developers paid off politicians to avoid adhering to city building codes, thereby allowing them to construct houses that were cheap but unsafe. The Department of Investigations came across a city worker who had not reported for work once in the previous eleven years. In all, during Fiorello's initial three years, the Department of Investigations terminated ninety-four city officials, twenty of whom were eventually imprisoned. Other departments also ferreted out corruption. McCormick's corrections department, for example, found that at one of the city's prisons, prisoners with political connections virtually ran the jail and served their sentences in comfort. McCormick changed this practice quickly and decisively by arresting the deputy warden.

In other cases it was not corruption but inefficiency that was the problem. Savings were achieved in a number of departments by eliminating shoddy practices and equipment.

In the sanitation department, the purchase department, the corporation counsel's office and others, new people and new techniques brought a smoother-running city government.

La Guardia insisted on absolute honesty among his people. An individual who was on a personal crusade to clean up New York, he continued his lifelong commitment to ethical government and imposed harsh penalties on anyone who violated his code. His bent toward good government is evident in a number of instances. Immediately upon taking office, for example, he ordered that no Christmas gifts were to be exchanged within departments so that city workers would not be forced to give presents to superiors in exchange for possible favors. He demanded that city stationery be used only for official city business. On one occasion, he issued a memorandum noting that he had in front of him "a letter soliciting funds for a very worthy public service. However, the merits of the cause will be no excuse for improper use of official stationery." Beyond these relatively trifling concerns, he was effective in cleaning up city departments, offering ethical management, and limiting corruption.

Corruption was never fully eliminated in the city bureaucracy (and probably never can be), but those who violated Fiorello's code of ethics felt his wrath. Ernest Cuneo tells the story of an acquaintance of the mayor who got a parking ticket from a young policeman. When the acquaintance refused to take the citation, he was arrested. When he complained to La Guardia, the mayor immediately called the station house. The captain of the precinct started to apologize for the incident, assuming that the mayor was angry about what had happened. Fiorello instead screamed at the captain for apologizing, praised the arresting officer for showing no favors, and sent him a box of cigars. La Guardia said that this was the type of cop he wanted on the force. In another situation, when two long-time workers in the Department of Public Works were involved in a small theft, La Guardia, in a letter to the department commissioner, said, "The age of these employees or the length of service in the city . . . makes no impression on me. In fact, it aggravates the case and would indicate that they have been too long in the city service. The fact that the value of the property was not very great likewise does not detract from the moral turpitude involved."

If commissioners refused to follow through on charges of dishonesty on their staffs, they too would be relieved of their jobs. In 1941, some oil burner inspectors in the fire department were charged with extorting money from companies that installed the burners. The department found one of the inspectors guilty instead of a lesser charge and let him off lightly. La Guardia was outraged. He dismissed the deputy fire commissioner who had been in charge of the departmental trial and had decided on the lesser charge, as well as the fire commissioner, who had agreed with his deputy. Perhaps in some instances La Guardia overreacted, but given the corruption that was the order of the day under Tammany, Fiorello probably thought he had to crack down hard to prevent the same situation in his administration. Similar to many of those in his fusion good-government group, La Guardia believed that his duty was to end the rule of corrupt politicians and criminals over New York.

The mayor got involved in all aspects of his administration, watching, controlling, and always seeking the limelight that he loved. As one magistrate stated, "It seemed as though the town had been invaded by an army of small, plump men in big hats; he was everywhere." He worked around the clock. If he came upon a traffic tie-up or a pothole on his drive to work, he immediately telephoned the appropriate commissioner to ask him to take care of the problem right away. He sometimes arrived unannounced at one of the municipal lodging houses for the poor, got in line, and saw for himself how the bureaucracy dealt with the city's unfortunate. In one case, he got in line at a relief station and found that the staff was not doing its job and that the director was late for work. He became enraged, made the staff speed up their interviewing of relief applicants, and fired some of the workers as well as the director. These impromptu inspections were frequent occurrences. La Guardia was concerned with the common people, how they were living, what their problems were. His concern was motivated by longstanding antipathy to "the interests," and his concern for the poor, and his desire to remain popular and stay in office. Like early progressives, he believed that government should make people's lives better, and he was fiercely determined that bureaucrats should do their jobs and serve the people. La Guardia waged war against corruption, indifference, and favoritism, the enemies of good government.

La Guardia showed a less admirable side of his character while in office. He could be egotistical, demanding, and abusive, with a quick temper and a willingness to humiliate subordinates. Some on his staff, such as Moses, would not tolerate such abuse and stood their ground until the mayor backed off. Others, however, crumbled under Fiorello's barrages of invective. He brought his commissioners together every so often to award a "prize" to the official who had made the biggest mistake since the last meeting. He was not one to pat others on the back for a good job; he simply expected it, and he would not tolerate mistakes from himself or his staff. As he said when hiring an aide on one occasion, "I'm very disagreeable. I'm inconsiderate. I expect you to do twice as much as can possibly be done, and . . . in half the time it is possible to do it." At times he would fire aides in an explosion of temper but would come in the next morning expecting them to be at work. Of course, sometimes the firings were legitimate. For the good of the city, Fiorello would dismiss friends if they could not handle their jobs. The city came first.

The mayor loved his work and felt that others should feel the same. He took few vacations and had little interest in luxuries or outside recreation. He wanted his commissioners to pay attention to every detail of their departments and be on top of every problem twenty-four hours a day. When his fire commissioner was in the hospital in 1940, La Guardia sent him a note instructing him "to resume the duties of Commissioner to the extent of your physical capabilities. This can be done from the hospital." City officials might get a call from the mayor at any time to discuss something or to summon them to a meeting. And they had to be available. When Fiorello was out of town, nothing changed. He would sometimes call his officials just to make sure they were on the job. He was a driven man who wanted to get a job done and had no tolerance for laziness or inefficiency.

Fiorello also, as in his earlier years, liked to dramatize his actions in order to make the public aware of what he was doing and what needed to be done. He would often rush off to fires wearing fire helmet, raincoat, and boots, claiming that he wanted to show the firemen that their mayor would not send them into a situation in which he would not go himself. On one occasion, Fiorello, who more than once showed his physical courage, ran into a restaurant that was on fire. He stayed until after the last fireman had left and came out covered with soot and said, "I gave the refrigeration system a personal going over. I wanted to find out whether the building code had been violated." He could be seen smashing slot machines with a sledge hammer in order to rid the city of crime, conducting the orchestra at a concert in the park, sitting at a judge's bench and sentencing gamblers, and appearing unexpectedly around the city to make sure laws were being enforced.

His unusual behavior had a purpose. Rexford Tugwell, a

New Deal advisor and La Guardia's chairman of the City Planning Commission, asserted that Fiorello used his dramatic style and even his temper to make a point and to make himself look good. It was good acting, according to Tugwell, that followed a technique used very well by Theodore Roosevelt to arouse public interest and bring attention to what he was doing. But it was more than good acting, as Tugwell indicates. He said that "the exploitation of the poor, the undermining of civil liberties, the corruption of public office, the pretensions of the rich or the noble, or the prostitution of democracy by would-be or actual dictators who held power by force—these were the causes that roused in him [La Guardia] a rage he was utterly unable to control." And if that rage also won votes, so much the better. He was at times too emotional for a politician, but his emotions, temper, resentments, competitiveness, and even his insensitivity were related to his desires to both improve the city and further his own career and status.

Historian Jordan Schwarz describes the mayor as "a puritan revolutionary in quest of his City upon a Hill, an incorruptible municipal government." This portrait is a fitting one for this ambitious, aggressive, workaholic, and honest administrator, who seemed more like the progressive mayors of earlier years (e. g., Toledo's Samuel "Golden Rule" Jones or Cleveland's Tom Johnson) than the mayors of the 1930s. Like La Guardia, these early reform mayors tried to eliminate inefficiency and corruption in their municipalities, run honest administrations, and develop social welfare programs. Fiorello, however, was able to pull together the progressive municipal ideals of the late nineteenth and early twentieth centuries with the new urban activism of the federal government in the New Deal period. This activism allowed La Guardia to utilize federal funds and power to create a more livable city and achieve goals that were beyond those of the previous reform mayors.

Economic Rebound

La Guardia wanted to deal with all of the city's problems, from health to racism to crime. However, his immediate concerns when taking office, other than rooting out corruption, were improving the financial condition of the city and responding to the depression. When Fiorello became mayor, the municipal budget was still unbalanced. Along with other factors, this resulted in a poor credit rating for New York, which made its municipal bonds difficult to sell. The unbalanced budget also prevented the city from securing federal (mainly Public Works Administration) money for various public works projects. New York also lacked sufficient funds for unemployment relief. La Guardia's initial economic priorities, then, were to reestablish a sound financial base for the city and to balance the budget in order to raise the city's credit rating.

He sought to accomplish these goals through an Emergency Economy Bill that would cut costs by streamlining the city bureaucracy and reducing salaries. As part of the plan, the mayor's powers would be enhanced for two years. La Guardia would have the authority to eliminate city and county agencies, supplant them with others, abolish jobs, cut salaries, impose up to one month of unpaid furloughs, and supersede state laws concerning the city. Eliminating, in particular, county offices meant that Democratic patronage positions would be cut, and therefore the Democrat-controlled Board of Aldermen was against that idea. Civil service workers opposed the wage cuts. Governor Lehman balked at the bill because it gave the mayor too much power. An amended bill finally passed the state legislature in April 1934 after earlier versions had failed to do so. Under the changed bill (in which the Board of Estimate, not the mayor, had enhanced power), city workers, except teachers, firemen, policemen and those with very low wages, but including the mayor, had their salaries reduced. (La Guardia was never interested in making money and willingly accepted a salary cut from $40,000 to $22,500. At his own request, his salary was not raised during his entire twelve years in office. La Guardia took this step even though he had virtually no savings or even a car when he was elected.) Some workers were fired or put on one-month unpaid furloughs (court personnel were exempted from the furloughs) and various city, but not county, agencies could be revamped. Although La Guardia was disappointed by the amendments put into his original proposal ("I awaited a big, healthy, bouncing child, and find a small, puny, anemic, undersized baby"), he used the final bill to improve the city's finances.

The effect of this legislation was to reduce the budget by $14 million, thereby cutting the projected 1934 deficit in half. However, the amended bill was not as effective as the initial legislation would have been in reducing government costs. As a result, new or raised taxes, including a sales tax that La Guardia had fought against in Congress, were temporarily imposed. These measures were taken because, as the mayor said, "I am looking to the 1935 and 1936 budgets too, and I don't want to go through the hell of these last three months again. I want a well-balanced budget so that I will be able to administer the affairs of the city efficiently and intelligently." The combination of the Economy Bill, new taxes, and Mayor O'Brien's earlier agreement with the bankers to cut the budget (with which La Guardia concurred), along with some new loans, enabled La Guardia to balance the budget in 1934. When that was accomplished, the banks were more willing to buy and more able to resell the city's bonds, and also were amenable to easing some of the Bankers Agreement provisions. The federal government was now willing to provide loans for public works. Interest rates on the bonds decreased as the city's credit rating rose. La Guardia's penchant at this time for saving money for the good of the city extended to all areas. He sent memos to his commissioners ordering them to make sure the lights were turned off in city offices when they were not in use and not to waste office supplies. Sometimes his concern about the city's economy extended too far. For example, following Tammany's earlier cost-cutting practice, he kept many qualified teachers at the lower-paying rank of substitute teacher although they worked at regular teacher hours and positions.

"Everyone Who Needs It Is Entitled to Relief"

With the finances in order, the mayor was able to turn his attention to his goals for the city. And he generally ran a positive, concerned government as noted in numerous instances. After inspecting the Women's House of Detention in 1935, he ordered that the visitors' areas be refurbished so as to create a better milieu for those coming to see the prisoners and that the prisoners be given more privacy in their cells. He requested that out-of-town runaways found in the city whose families could not afford their fares home should receive city money for the journey. On more significant issues, such as unemployment, Fiorello supported government relief for those out of work. "Everyone who needs it is entitled to relief. It is an obligation of those in need to apply for it," he said. Tammany had not administered the relief situation very well during the depths of the depression, 1931 to 1933. La Guardia set out to improve the system. In 1931, New York State had set up a procedure to provide relief to the unemployed who were not in poorhouses or workhouses. Although the state funded part of the home relief system, the city was responsible for raising most of the money and for overseeing its distribution through the city-run Home Relief Bureau. Although the federal government, with its Federal Emergency Relief Act, began to offer relief money starting in 1933, the city still had to raise funds as well as manage the relief process. Under Tammany, relief was funded at a low level, mainly through bonds rather than additional taxes, and was never developed on a sound financial footing. The allowance provided for food was minimal; rent assistance was offered irregularly, as was fuel assistance; and offices of the city's Home Relief Bureau at times had to shut their doors to avoid responding to additional relief appeals, for which the bureau had no money. Meanwhile, the number of needy in the city climbed. As of 1934, one family in seven was on relief, and professionals such as engineers and lawyers were now asking for aid.

Tammany had used relief for political gain, both in terms of the agency staff and those receiving relief. Loyal Democrats favored by the Tammany bosses received relief aid even if they did not deserve it. Without political connections, however, the needy often could not get help. The whole relief process changed under La Guardia. He funded the system with new taxes, thereby furnishing the bureau with sufficient money. An adequate source of funds allowed the bureau to provide regular stipends to those receiving relief money (under Tammany, payments sometimes skipped weeks); to augment the money for food as costs increased; and to offer regular payments for rent, fuel, and various other necessities. La Guardia did not use the relief process for political gain. During his administration, New York's relief system not only functioned better financially, but also did more to help people through their personal economic crises. As the relief system grew under La Guardia and the federal Works Progress Administration (WPA), however, it was far from perfect. Sometimes money was wasted and worthless projects were funded. But the system also reached out to many, and it was innovative. New York City WPA administrator Victor Ridder, appointed largely because of La Guardia's appeal to the president, set up a special women's unit to improve its outreach to the unemployed. Once again, Fiorello's approach was to uplift those who were down and out, speak for the unfortunate, and respond to the needs of people in trouble.

Building a New City

Relief aid included creating federally funded jobs, mainly through public works projects. With the help of Adolf Berle, who had close ties to Roosevelt and who became La Guardia's liaison with the president, Civil Works Administration (CWA) and PWA money flowed into the city. Using federal funds and/or city money, La Guardia, with Robert Moses, rebuilt New York during his years in office. The Triborough Bridge connecting Manhattan, the Bronx, and Queens was completed; the West Side Highway was expanded and other highways were built; the Holland Tunnel was constructed and work on the Brooklyn-Battery Tunnel was started; the subway system was enlarged; new schools, hospitals, parks, and housing were constructed; new sewage disposal plants were built that helped eliminate the pollution of rivers and beach areas; and two airports were developed (one did not open until 1948). This rebuilding of the city also helped ease unemployment as people were put to work on these projects.

La Guardia's skill in securing money was due largely to his willingness to seek federal funds and his New Deal connections. His ties to the New Deal were strong, based on his congressional support for Roosevelt's programs and his help in developing the CWA in late 1933, before taking office as mayor. His good relationship with Roosevelt, Harry Hopkins (director of the Federal Emergency Relief Administration, the Civil Works Administration and, later, the Works Progress Administration), and Harold Ickes (secretary of the interior and head of the PWA) and an ability to develop project proposals to submit for consideration as soon as federal programs were started reaped enormous benefits. Roosevelt remarked in 1940, "Our Mayor is probably the most appealing person I know. He comes to Washington and tells me a sad story. The tears run down my cheeks and tears run down his cheeks and the first thing I know he has wrangled another $50,000,000." Rather than having to depend solely on the state, La Guardia was able to fund New York City development through federal government largesse. It is clear that this new federal-city cooperation, which gave Fiorello the means to accomplish much more than earlier mayors, was partly responsible for his successes as New York's chief administrator.

New York was at times the first to receive federal money and often in substantial amounts. For example, even before the WPA was officially established, the mayor had a list of projects planned and waiting for WPA funds. This efficiency enabled New York to be one of the few cities to secure work for the unemployed as soon as the federal program was set up in 1935. New York City was also given an independent WPA program that was separate from the state, the only city to receive such special handling. Of course, because of its size New York had special problems; however, its treatment by the federal government resulted in large part from La Guardia's ties to Roosevelt and his efficient and honest management of city and federal funds. The mayor's good-government goals fit in well with New Deal aims as he replaced unqualified Tammany hacks in local New Deal agencies with people who could do the job.

The mayor turned to experts to rebuild the city: engineers and planners, not politicians, developed new ideas. Moses, of course, was the expert of experts in getting public projects built. As La Guardia's parks commissioner and simultaneously head of the State Parks Commission, Moses wielded tremendous power and was able to push through his plans. Moses also took over as head of the Triborough Bridge Authority in order to complete work, long stalled by Tammany inefficiency and corruption, on this massive bridge project. His power expanded as he secured control over still other positions involving public projects. The commissioner, whose personality was much like La Guardia's, often clashed with the mayor. Both had to be in control and had great work to fulfill. Despite their conflicts, which resulted in some epic battles, La Guardia stood behind his commissioner and defended him against his opponents (including Roosevelt, who had a personal feud with Moses).

Fiorello was willing to overlook the criticism of Moses's work. For example, the parks commissioner's grand design for New York absorbed a good deal of funds that could have gone to physical plant maintenance or the building of more health-care centers and libraries. Moses improved New York but only according to his own vision, and with his usual self-confidence and arrogance, he was unwilling to listen to any alternative plan. Faced with criticism, he dug his heels in and pushed harder for his programs. He was sure he knew what was best for New York. On more than one occasion, Moses's beloved highways destroyed well-functioning neighborhoods, such as Brooklyn's Sunset Park. Nonetheless, La Guardia saw mainly Moses's accomplishments, which provided New York with the public projects that mayors like to point to with pride, especially during election campaigns. The bottom line was that Moses finished what he set out to do. He built a new New York, with such amenities as new parks, playgrounds, highways, and bridges, and therefore La Guardia was inclined to disregard the personality clashes and other disputes. Fiorello truly loved the city—from the skyscrapers of midtown Manhattan to the tenements of Harlem and the South Bronx to the suburban-style houses of Queens—and wanted to improve it. According to one of his aides, the mayor enjoyed riding around the city on Sundays in order to get new ideas on what else to build for the people. He saw Moses as the one man who could make improvements quickly and efficiently.

Decent, affordable housing for New York's citizens was the mayor's special concern. His interest in building new housing resulted partly from the earlier tragedy involving his wife and daughter, and partly to the need to find jobs for the unemployed. New York was filled with dilapidated housing through which fires often raged. Crime, disease, and general human misery were rampant in the city's slums. Conditions worsened during the depression as poverty mounted. Along with other reformers, La Guardia felt morally compelled to act. Working with New Deal officials, and fulfilling the dreams of many earlier housing reformers, Fiorello started to clear the slums and build safe, well-constructed public housing. Initially, because of financial and other problems, some old housing was renovated rather than destroyed. For example, the city's initial project was Manhattan's First Houses, which opened in 1935 and combined renovated and newly constructed buildings on the Lower East Side. The massive slum clearance and rebuilding projects would come later.

Among the public housing projects developed were the Williamsburg, Red Hook, and Kingsborough Houses in Brooklyn; Manhattan's Vladeck, Harlem River, and East River Houses; Queens's South Jamaica and Queensbridge Houses; the Clason Point Houses in the Bronx and others. In all, thirteen projects were built that housed the city's working poor and provided employment for thousands. The public housing system, however, had its problems. Some of the projects were racially segregated. And the down-and-out poor, those on relief and without jobs, simply could not get apartments; tenants were meticulously picked to ensure that they would pay the rent on time and had good personal habits. However, this imperfect system was better than nothing, and New York needed housing and jobs.

Although the federal government often hesitated as it took its first steps towards slum clearance and public housing, La Guardia was able to accomplish a lot. Certainly the New Deal's expanded government role and funding, together with La Guardia's municipal reform and progressive vision, gave the city a new look in many ways. And Fiorello's efforts to secure federal aid for New York helped to bring the plight of all cities to Roosevelt's attention. La Guardia became a spokesman not only for New York, but for other American cities as well. In 1935 he was chosen president of the newly formed U.S. Conference of Mayors. La Guardia was the leading advocate of strengthening ties between the federal and city governments, and thereby established a new relationship between the two.

A Bold Leader

La Guardia was, as ever, bold in his approach; he was in every way the strong leader the early progressives had envisioned who was willing to expand government power. A good example of this style of governing is an incident involving one of La Guardia's pet interests—public utilities. He was concerned that the electric companies were overcharging both the city and private consumers, and that prices were increasing. He refused to accept the price rise; instead, he made plans in 1934 and again in 1935 to construct a city-owned power plant. Like the New Deal's Tennessee Valley Authority, this plant would not only provide electricity but also would help to determine whether the private companies were charging fair rates. This threat to compete with the private electric companies by selling electricity at a lower rate convinced the private companies to reduce their rates both to the city and to the private citizen. Fiorello then called off his plans to develop a power plant. According to one of his close advisors, he never had a realistic hope of building it; he simply wanted some leverage over the private companies. La Guardia also showed his innovative leadership in his successful attempt in 1940, after years of effort, to consolidate the public and private subway and other transportation systems in the city under a city-owned and -managed operation. Seabury, who had long been interested in municipal-ownership issues, was active in bringing about this consolidation, which enhanced the efficiency of the transit system.

Centralization of city functions to improve government efficiency, also a progressive goal, was obvious not only in transit unification, but in various other city departments as well. Tammany had long fought consolidation of county and city agencies, because the more government offices there were, the more patronage was available. Under La Guardia, the five borough park departments were brought together in one city department under Robert Moses. The same process was used for the public works department, the office of sheriff, and other city agencies.

In some cases the mayor appeared to break with earlier progressive policies, such as support for unions. But here too there was actually a continuity to La Guardia's actions and beliefs. He was a strong advocate of unions, a closed shop (in which workers in a business establishment had to join the union in order to get and keep their jobs), and particularly the right to picket and strike. However, this architect of the Norris–La Guardia Act did not accept the right of workers to endanger the public safety in order to win their demands. He was particularly adamant on this point in regard to city government workers. For example, La Guardia opposed the closed shop for city workers, and did not support their right to strike, believing that a strike by closed-shop government employees could deny crucial services to the public. Besides, he did not think that the city's personnel needed to strike or even join a union, because civil service regulations protected them.

On a few occasions he worked dramatically to end strikes

that he felt threatened the public welfare. When building service workers went on strike, leaving many New Yorkers without heat in their apartments, La Guardia called the union officials to a meeting at City Hall. After he got them together in a room, he left, bolted the door so they could not get out, and shut off the heat. The cold room gave the officials a good idea of what other New Yorkers were facing during the strike, and they quickly agreed to a settlement. La Guardia also was willing to use the police against violent strikes, although he was accused of waiting too long when a 1934 taxi drivers' strike turned violent. La Guardia had told the police when he took office not to interfere with peaceful picketing and the right of free speech. Although he was reluctant to break with that statement, he did so in this case when he became convinced that violence was occurring. That the mayor could take action against unions indicates some flexibility not always seen in his career. But it did not really matter if the "interests" represented abusive corporations or bullying and violent unions. If the common citizen was threatened in any way, La Guardia came to the rescue. This concept could be observed early in his career. In 1925, for example, La Guardia had responded to a coal strike by backing a law that would allow federal money to be used to buy coal overseas, thereby safeguarding the public from a coal shortage during the winter. He was consistent in his belief that the public safety came first.

However, the mayor's goal for unions was not to force them back to work. Rather, he spent much time trying to settle strikes and avoid disputes. Although he could be a hothead on certain matters, he also could be the epitome of an impartial and unemotional mediator. He believed in negotiation and voluntary arbitration of labor disputes and was responsible for setting up the city's Industrial Relations Board in 1936. This board, with its city-appointed impartial arbitrators and mediators, worked to settle labor-management conflict in a peaceful fashion. In 1937 the state took over its functions. Clearly, Fiorello was drawing from his own union experiences in developing his mayoral policies. As a labor lawyer, beginning with the 1912 garment strike, as a prounion congressman who often ran with labor support, and as an impartial arbitrator for the Associated Dress Industries of America in 1933 before the mayoral election, he gained substantial knowledge of worker-boss relations and was effective in settling many disputes.

An Explosion in Harlem

The mayor's efficient management of the city, his concern for the public welfare, and his energy and honesty made him a popular figure in New York and maintained his national reputation as a progressive leader. However, there were problems in the city during his tenure. Ethnic issues continued to be important and often divisive; La Guardia, by necessity and design, often found himself deeply involved in New York's ethnic warfare.

Indicative of problems in New York's multicultural world was the Harlem riot of 1935. Harlem had seen a large increase in its black population during and after World War I. Thousands of poor blacks from the South poured into the community, putting an immediate strain on the neighborhood. Faced with discrimination in housing and employment, deteriorating living conditions, and growing social problems, Harlem's blacks faced difficult times during the 1920s. The depression exacerbated already serious problems and pushed the community into further economic distress. By the mid-1930s, the community, frustrated and angry, was ripe for an explosion. The spark for the riot that took place in March 1935 was a rumor that a black child had been beaten and killed after shoplifting in a local store, allegedly by the police and the store manager, who were white. In fact, no child had died or been beaten. However, the violence engendered by the rumor lasted two days, consisting mainly of the breaking of windows at white-owned stores, looting, and physical assaults. The riot clearly revealed the tensions and frustrations in a community that had been devastated by the depression and tormented by continued discrimination. La Guardia's response was to set up a biracial (six blacks and five whites) Mayor's Commission on Conditions in Harlem to determine the causes of the riot. The commission was broken down into subcommittees that dealt with housing and recreation, health care, crime and law enforcement, education, employment, and relief discrimination. This commission produced a devastating report that noted such problems as police brutality; discrimination in the relief structure, city departments, and private industry; unemployment; high prices and inferior products in Harlem stores; and general inequality in health care, education, and housing.

The report was critical of various city commissioners and departments and, by implication, also of the mayor. La Guardia, always sensitive to criticism and unfavorable newspaper coverage, did not release the report, which nonetheless was leaked to the press. He also did not follow all of its recommendations or that of a follow-up study, particularly in regard to the suggested firing of some of his commissioners. However, the mayor was concerned with conditions in the area, had responded to some community needs even before the riot, and was to make even more efforts to improve life in Harlem afterward. La Guardia sympathized with the problems of his black constituents and also did not want to lose the important black vote. Before the riot, he had already supported the building of the Harlem River Houses, a federal project. After the riot, the mayor stepped up his efforts in this section of the city. Other structures went up within the next few years, such as

a women's pavilion for Harlem Hospital, a central Harlem
health center, and two new schools, the first to be built in
Harlem in over two decades.

La Guardia attempted to rectify longstanding problems
of discrimination in city departments and in the relief system. Blacks were underrepresented on work relief projects, given the percentage of this group that was out of
work but employable, and even when on work relief were
given low-paying positions. Black doctors and nurses were
discriminated against in hospitals throughout the city,
including Harlem Hospital, which was in their own community. In fact, it was not until 1925, during Tammany's tenure, that five black doctors were allowed to practice at
Harlem Hospital as visiting doctors. Mayor Walker's appointment in the late 1920s of black Democratic leader Ferdinand Q. Morton as head of the Civil Service Commission
improved conditions slightly. More black doctors, but only
Democrats, were brought into the hospital. However, Tammany only skimmed the surface of the rampant racial discrimination in the city and Morton's power was limited.

La Guardia brought more substantial changes and progress in the aftermath of the riots, though clearly the problem of racism persisted. For the first time a black woman
became a school principal; more blacks were appointed to
the Emergency Relief Bureau staff, including a significant
number of executive positions (supervisors, investigators);
two new relief bureaus were opened in Harlem; more
blacks were appointed to the medical board of Harlem
Hospital; and the city's hospital department, one of the
agencies criticized in the commission report, hired additional black nurses, attendants, and doctors and placed
them in hospitals that had had discriminatory policies. La
Guardia also did not allow unions that barred blacks to represent the city's subway workers in collective bargaining
with his administration. Thus, some change was evident in
the increase of blacks in various city positions, the opening

up of civil service to more blacks, more frequent appear-
ances by La Guardia before black groups, and a speeded-
up effort to secure PWA funding, applied for earlier, to
upgrade Harlem Hospital. But because the black community had been so badly neglected for many years and faced
a persistent discrimination that La Guardia could not root
out, conditions did not greatly improve.

Although the depression and Roosevelt's inattention to
black needs exacerbated the plight of New York's black citizens, La Guardia too must bear some blame. Although
Fiorello took a sincere interest in the black community and
conferred often with black leaders, his personality, mana-
gerial abilities, and belief system interfered with a more
thoroughgoing response. An unwillingness to accept critical comment and at times a naive trust in the good faith of
his commissioners precluded the necessary input from
more knowledgeable and impartial sources that would
have helped the mayor avoid mistakes. Racism, for example, continued in the hospital department and in the
city's hospitals after the riot in part because of the mayor's
willingness to allow city commissioners to conduct their
own in-house investigations of complaints.

La Guardia did not seem to understand the depth of racism in American society, and believed that blacks, like Jews,
Italians, and the Irish, would be able to overcome discrimination and problems through self-improvement and by im-
pressing the rest of society with their worth. Fiorello felt
that ethnic communities should clean "their own house[s]"
and thereby provide even bigots with little to criticize, thus
causing discrimination to wane. The road to a harmonious
society, he believed, was largely based on the group's own
actions. New legislation to enforce tolerance would not
work; instead, existing rights should be guaranteed and re-
affirmed. La Guardia, who thought the white ethnics had
assimilated well and dealt with the hostility against them,
saw blacks as just another group in America's melting pot

whose problems would fade when employment opportunity was provided, rights were protected, and acceptance was won through group improvement and hard work. Although not fully understanding the strength and longevity of race prejudice in America, La Guardia's support for equal opportunity and tolerance, and his usual defense of all minorities against attack speaks well for him. However, he did have his failings which became evident a few years later during World War II.

Responding to Hitler and Mussolini

As a politician he used ethnic fears, hopes, and desires to win votes but often these campaign tactics represented his own beliefs as well. The appointment of a black or Italian served two roles as did his persistent attacks on the Nazi regime in Germany. During a decade that led to the horrors of the Holocaust and saw Nazis marching not only in Berlin but also in New York (which had a branch of the German-American Bund, a Nazi organization based in the United States and made up mostly of recent German immigrants), it was important for political leaders to speak out against the rising tide of terror in the world. La Guardia did so to a greater degree than did many other public figures. Nazism, of course, represented all that was reprehensible to him, with its dictatorial structure, elimination of personal freedom, and horrendous abuse of the Jewish population. The Third Reich mirrored the forces Fiorello had long fought against in this country—the narrow-minded, bigoted, greedy "interests" who cheated and abused the weaker elements in society. The way to eliminate the wrongdoing, in the tradition of the early progressive muckrakers, was to expose it to public view and allow the expected moral outrage to deal with the problem. La Guardia as a committed progressive and advocate of the new immigrant groups surely felt this way although a desire to win votes and be the center of attention also served as strong motivations to speak out.

A solely progressive-based opposition to dictators, however, would have included a public denunciation of Mussolini, but until 1940 La Guardia was publicly silent on Italy's Fascist ruler. He fought against the Italian supporters of fascism in the Sons of Italy as early as the 1920s and initially served as grand master of the anti-Fascist New York State chapter of the group, which split from the national organization. But he remained, among prominent anti-Fascists such as Luigi Antonini of the International Ladies Garment Workers Union (ILGWU) and Salvatore Cotillo, oddly quiet about the Italian dictator. He also, at times, tried to play both sides of the fence. In 1935, the mayor attended a concert that was staged to allow Italian-Americans to show their support for Fascist Italy. Although he had been warned about what his presence at the concert would indicate, La Guardia insisted on going, much to the chagrin of anti-Fascists. However, when Italy's anti-Semitic decrees were issued in 1938, Fiorello was one of a number of Italian-American leaders who voiced their disapproval. Yet, he did not directly and publicly criticize Mussolini until Italy entered World War II on the side of Germany in June 1940. La Guardia was an ambitious politician who fought for his beliefs, sometimes against great odds, but not when it would clearly lose significant numbers of votes for him and gain little in return. Although he was privately antagonistic to Mussolini, he would have derived no benefit from an early public denunciation of this dictator, who remained popular in New York's Italian-American neighborhoods until Italy's entry into the war.

His attacks on Hitler and the Nazis, however, represented a perfect convergence of belief and political ambition. He first lambasted Nazi racial policies in May 1933 and continued throughout the decade to assail that reprehensible government and also, along with other politicians, to make nazism a political issue in New York. He also knew how to get the German government angry, which drew support to the mayor and made good press. On one occasion, as the mayor's advisor Newbold Morris relates, Fiorello provided a visiting Nazi delegation with "an escort of Jewish policemen" to take them around the city. Morris notes that when the Nazis realized how the mayor had made fools of them and their ideology, their reaction "was unprintable."

More seriously, one of La Guardia's responses to nazism was to advocate a boycott of German goods. Supported by various Jewish organizations, the boycott began slowly in March 1933 as part of the effort to indicate displeasure with Nazi policies. It emerged fully as a tactic a month later after Jewish businesses were boycotted in Germany. La Guardia became vice-chairman of the Non-Sectarian Anti-Nazi League to Champion Human Rights, one of the main boycott organizations. La Guardia's willingness to take an important and symbolic position in the boycott effort was encouraging to the many Americans who wanted to register strong disapproval of Nazi Germany's policies. And, of course, Jewish Americans were grateful to have someone of La Guardia's prominence join the fight against Hitler. Some German-Americans were concerned that there would be a repeat of the anti-German hysteria of World War I and disapproved of the boycott, fearing that it would turn into a weapon against them instead of Germany. German-Americans, however, had seen their political power decline sharply since 1917. Like the Irish, they represented the old immigrants, and were no longer of any great concern to a politician who identified with the ascendant newer groups. A public response to nazism, even if it cost La Guardia some German support, could still be an effective vote-gathering tool.

As in the Fama incident, where a single individual's case

had revealed the mayor's attitudes toward an older group, in 1935 La Guardia indicated his feelings once again in a situation involving a newly arrived German immigrant. Conditions for Jews in Germany had worsened by this time and the mayor, in a dramatic show of protest against Germany, refused to grant a masseur operator's license to Paul Kress, an immigrant from Germany who indicated no plans to become a U.S. citizen. La Guardia noted that as long as American Jews faced discrimination in Germany, German nationals would receive no help here. The issue actually concerned a Treaty of Commerce and Friendship signed in 1925 between the United States and Germany in which the countries agreed that citizens of one country could pursue their occupations unhampered in the other country.

Although there were protests from a number of German-American organizations in New York (of which some were pro-Nazi); from Victor Ridder (soon to be WPA administrator for the city and publisher of the *New Yorker Staats-Zeitung*), who had known La Guardia since his 1916 congressional campaign; and even from many Jewish leaders, who did not think it was fair for Kress to be singled out and did not feel that Jews in Germany would benefit from this action, the mayor would not relent. Fiorello was also told by his legal advisor that his refusal to issue a license, thereby violating the 1925 treaty, was not legal. Mayors did not have any authority to break treaties even if, as Fiorello claimed, the Germans broke the treaty first. According to the State Department, the treaty was still operative and the mayor was legally bound to provide the license. He still refused. La Guardia said in 1936, "I run the subways, and he [Secretary of State Cordell Hull] runs the state department—except when I abrogate a treaty or something." Kress finally went back to Germany, thus terminating the conflict. Here was the mayor in a very common stance—

grandstanding, dramatizing an event, personalizing an issue, fighting for his convictions, and winning votes. It was a style that constantly made him a controversial figure.

Progressive Politics

Not only ethnicity, but also progressive politics kept La Guardia in the limelight as a controversial political leader. A Republican New Dealer who continued to fight Tammany (which still was a formidable opponent), Fiorello remained a maverick, unwilling to be controlled by either party. His political interest at this time lay in developing a new Progressive party. He actually thought, according to Tugwell, that by 1940 the Republicans and Democrats would be replaced by Conservative and Progressive parties. His desires in this direction were matched by other progressives. Senator Robert La Follette, Jr., a Republican from Wisconsin, who continued his father's progressive politics in the Senate, thought that the depression would cause a political reorganization. Governor Philip La Follette of Wisconsin, his younger brother, saw the possibility of a left-wing third party by 1940. Fiorello envisaged that progressive Republicans (such as the La Follettes and Norris) and New Deal Democrats would merge politically, as would conservatives from Republican and Democratic ranks. In fact, it already appeared to be happening: A national meeting of progressives, which La Guardia helped organize, was held in September 1936 and endorsed Roosevelt for president; progressive Republicans were supportive of Roosevelt's reelection in 1936; a Progressive party had been reestablished in Wisconsin in 1934 and could serve as the vanguard of the realignment; and in New York in 1936 the American Labor party (ALP) was formed. The ALP was organized in order to secure Democratic votes for Roosevelt without depending on the Tammany machine; it also would provide an alternative line on the ballot for those who supported Roosevelt but did not want to vote Democratic. The new party was set up with Roosevelt's approval and with considerable union involvement. The ALP represented itself as a leader of the political reorganization occurring in the country and as a progressive voice for the common man.

La Guardia was deeply involved in the formation of this party and soon voiced his willingness to vote the ALP ticket. It seemed to be the perfect political vehicle for the mayor. It represented La Guardia's concerns, attracted support from labor and from such New Deal Democrats as Senator Wagner and Governor Lehman, and drew in other maverick politicians, such as Marcantonio. In all, the ALP appeared to be the ideal organization to effect a national political realignment. In fact, according to Tugwell, La Guardia even thought that the ALP could catapult him into the presidency in 1940 as the leader of the nation's progressive elements, following Roosevelt's expected retirement after two terms. The ALP, meanwhile, would provide the mayor with another line on the ballot in case he lost Republican support in his 1937 bid for reelection. One contemporary political observer even suggested that some of Roosevelt's interest in a new party stemmed from his wish to provide Fiorello with a political organization for his 1937 contest. The president apparently saw La Guardia as the New Deal's voice in New York and wanted to keep him in office.

La Guardia had completed a successful first term, but still faced formidable opposition to his reelection. No fusion reformer had ever won a second term in New York. La Guardia set out to beat the odds.

CHAPTER FIVE

Reelection and Disappointment

The mayor's ambition, contentious nature, and convictions were the sources both of his success and his failure. He desired much, fought hard, and believed strongly. He continued to win the support of many New Yorkers and to antagonize many as well. His next eight years in office were to be rocky ones.

"He Is Our S.O.B.": The 1937 Campaign

La Guardia's lack of support for Republican presidential candidates (he backed FDR in his four campaigns for the White House), his unwillingness to provide much patronage to party leaders, and his political philosophy, which often was at odds with the conservative elements of the party, made the mayor worried about keeping Republican backing as 1937 approached. And he felt he needed the Republicans to win reelection. La Guardia had the support of some Republican leaders, and the party had in him a proven vote-getter who perhaps could pull other Republicans into office on his coattails. Kenneth Simpson, New York County Republican leader, said about Fiorello, "Yes, he is an S.O.B. . . . but he is *our* S.O.B., we must stick with him for the good of the party." Nonetheless, Fiorello faced a primary fight for the Republican nomination in 1937.

Only after defeating Royal S. Copeland, an anti-New Deal U.S. senator and a Democrat backed by Al Smith, did the mayor secure his spot on the Republican ticket. Therefore, La Guardia ran in 1937 on the Republican, ALP, City Fusion, and Progressive tickets. (The Progressive party was an outgrowth of the Progressive National Committee Supporting FDR for President, which had been formed in 1936.)

The mayor faced Democratic candidate and New York Supreme Court justice Jeremiah T. Mahoney in 1937. Mahoney, a Tammany district leader, had won a primary fight against Tammany's choice, Senator Copeland (who ran in both the Republican and Democratic primaries). Mahoney was the favorite of the political machines of all the boroughs except Manhattan. Flynn's Bronx machine and Frank Kelly's Brooklyn machine clearly were asserting themselves against Tammany control.

Ethnic issues dominated this campaign. As the 1937 election approached, La Guardia once again threw himself into the fray over nazism. In a speech in March of 1937 before the Women's Division of the American Jewish Congress, the mayor suggested that he would place Hitler's figure within a Chamber of Horrors at the planned New York World's Fair. Lashing out at the Nazi government and its fanatic leader, La Guardia again became the center of attention. A number of German-American groups protested, one questioning why the mayor has not recommended that Mussolini's figure also be placed in the Chamber of Horrors.

The Nazi issue continued to play a role in the 1937 election. As in La Guardia's other political campaigns, it was the opposition that first raised the ethnic issue in the actual campaign. The Democrats had nominated Jeremiah Mahoney partially because, as president of the Amateur Athletic Union, he had taken a stand against holding the 1936 Olympics in Berlin and had opposed U.S. participation if the games were held there. The Democrats hoped that Mahoney could therefore draw Jewish votes away from La Guardia.

Searching for a way to secure Jewish support, the Democrats repeatedly lashed out at the mayor for not doing enough to fight nazism and anti-Semitism in New York. The issue captured attention, however, only a few days before the election, when the German-American Bund planned a parade in Manhattan. The police had granted them a parade permit, and the Democrats blamed La Guardia, as head of the city government, for granting the permit. Using a prominent Mahoney supporter who was Jewish as spokesman, the Democrats accused La Guardia of allowing the parade in order to win Nazi votes or to use the incident politically by stopping the parade at the last minute and thereby attracting Jewish attention and support. One Mahoney pamphlet claimed that "La Guardia Today Sold Out to the NAZIS!" The mayor, according to an editorial in the *Day*, a Jewish newspaper supporting Mahoney, was giving New York the spectacle of a Nazi parade with uniforms and flags.

The mayor's response reflected his desire to hold onto his Jewish vote while remaining true to his belief in constitutional rights. La Guardia first said that he had not been involved in granting the parade permit. He also suggested that perhaps Tammany had been behind the whole incident, in hopes that a Nazi parade would hurt the mayor politically. There also was some evidence that the Democrats were trying to provoke a violent clash at the parade between the Nazis and the Jewish War Veterans group to further embarrass the mayor. La Guardia held his ground; he allowed the parade but restricted the route and did not allow the Nazis to don their uniforms or sing their songs. In this way the mayor, a strong supporter of free speech and the right of assembly, gave the Nazis their constitutional rights but limited the shock value and offensiveness of their parade. It does not appear that La Guardia lost many Jewish votes because of this incident.

The Democrats made other ethnic appeals. They attacked La Guardia as a Communist and suggested that Catholic voters and particularly Irish Catholics had to defeat La Guardia on this issue. They accused the mayor of anti-Irish bigotry. They targeted Italian voters with arguments that La Guardia had not done enough to elevate their community and that only the Democrats could give the Italians the important positions they desired. The Democrats, more than the mayor, tried to use ethnic appeals and ethnic fears to win votes.

However, at this time La Guardia was too popular among Italians and Jews to lose. His effective management of the city combined with his support for Jewish, Italian, and black interests put him in a strong position for reelection. Mahoney was never able to effectively challenge the fact that La Guardia had done a good job, and he lashed out in vain at tax increases, the mayor's management abilities, and other concerns. The public was apprehensive about possible revival of Democratic machine power at City Hall and generally felt that Fiorello had done a good job. Also Roosevelt, although officially neutral in this campaign, tacitly supported La Guardia by inviting him to Washington for talks on various issues. Being seen with Roosevelt helped solidify Fiorello's support and demonstrated how important the national administration considered him to be.

As expected, La Guardia secured a big victory (1,344,016 votes to Mahoney's 889,581), winning 60.1 percent of the total vote. He took 68.6 percent of the vote in Jewish election districts and 62.6 percent in Italian districts; his strategy of pinning the election on Jewish and Italian support was effective. In the predominantly black Twenty-first Assembly District in Manhattan, La Guardia took 68.4 percent of the votes; his efforts to support the aspirations of black New Yorkers bore fruit. In contrast, in Irish election districts Mahoney won 63.2 percent of the vote, indicating that Irish ties to the Democrats and concern over charges of communism and anti-Irish attitudes in La Guardia's administration played an important role in putting this community in the Democratic camp. Mahoney also won in German election districts, with 53.2 percent of the vote. For many years, La Guardia had been sympathetic to Italian and Jewish concerns and therefore was able to speak to their needs and win their votes no matter what the Democrats said or did.

La Guardia became the first fusion reform mayor to be reelected in the city. Prior to 1937, reform mayors had lasted only one term; although their fusion slates had been strong enough to defeat Tammany initially, their organizations soon became fragmented and the public grew tired of them by the next election. Tammany was always able to rebound quickly. La Guardia changed this pattern through his ability to build an organization of his own with his F. H. La Guardia Political Club and his success in maintaining the public's interest in what he was doing. His skill in getting headlines, and his dramatic flair, political acumen, and ethnic and reform ties kept Tammany at bay. Boss Flynn called La Guardia one of the most astute politicians he had ever known. Until La Guardia, no other reformer had the political abilities of the wiliest machine candidates.

Stronger Than Ever

The 1937 victory should have been a political turning point for the mayor. He was internationally known, a prominent progressive, and a friend of Roosevelt. Having won in all five boroughs and having secured a majority on the Board of Estimate, Fiorello was stronger than ever. A new city charter that was adopted in 1936 and went into effect on January 1, 1938, replaced the Board of Aldermen with a smaller city council elected on the basis of proportional representation. Proportional representation was a progressive reform system in which voters in each borough ranked the candidates in order of preference on their ballots. Each first-choice candidate who received 75,000 votes would be elected. Any votes over 75,000 that the first-choice candidate received would be given to the ballot's second choice. This process would continue through third, fourth, and subsequent choices until no other candidate received 75,000 votes.

This system strengthened the presence of minor parties on the council and weakened the Democratic machines. Machine Democrats had controlled the Board of Aldermen partly because of their ability to redraw the aldermanic district boundaries to their benefit. The new council eliminated these districts, created boroughwide districts, had its candidates chosen by petition (rather than by a primary in machine-run nominating elections), and thereby provided for a more representative government. The last Board of Aldermen was almost completely in Democratic machine hands, (with sixty-two positions out of a total of sixty-five). In the first city council, however, the Democratic organizations won just thirteen out of twenty-six seats; the rest went to antimachine Democrats, Republicans, City Fusion party members, ALP members, and independents. Under the aldermanic system, the Democrats, in the final election for the board, secured 66 percent of the vote but won 95 percent of the positions. In the first council election in November 1937, the Democratic machines secured 47 percent of the vote and received half of the council positions. The ALP, with a 21 percent vote, secured 19 percent of the council positions. The percentage of council seats for each party was now more in line with the votes won by that party's candidates.

The charter also enhanced the mayor's power and responsibilities and provided for a deputy mayor to deal with official but unimportant chores in order to ease the burden of office. La Guardia offered this position to Henry Curran. He accepted, but the mayor, a confirmed workaholic, gave his deputy little to do, and the position was budgeted out of existence in 1939. Some restructuring of city departments also took place under the new charter. For example, a City Planning Commission was created. A new Department of Housing and Buildings was set up to function in place of the separate borough buildings departments and the citywide tenement house department. Changes in other departments also streamlined city government. Although the charter was far from everything the progressives had wanted, it was a step in the right direction. La Guardia, therefore, had not only beaten the Democratic machines twice, but also continued to secure favorable publicity by presiding over a more efficient, reform-oriented city government.

La Guardia's second term was filled with more accomplishments. To improve public health, he built district health centers around the city. Fiorello's interest in aviation, which was evident even before his World War I heroics, combined with his desire to improve New York, led to the opening of an airport for the city in 1939. La Guardia considered a modern airport to be essential for any great and growing city. In recognition of Fiorello's contribution to the creation of the airport, political supporters and opponents alike agreed that it should be called La Guardia Field. In the same year that the airport opened, New York was host to the World's Fair, and La Guardia was fervently involved in the publicity and activity that went into its development and operation. The next year, La Guardia managed to unify the transit system in New York, an objective of a number of previous administrations.

Yet, even with these notable accomplishments, La Guardia in his second administration had less to keep him occupied and therefore was discontent. He had fulfilled many of his great goals for the city with regard to finances, re-

building, welfare, and corruption. Determined not to fall
into a humdrum routine, La Guardia strove always to do
more, and to keep active on the big problems of the day.
His energy needed other outlets.

Reaching for More

An ambitious politician who sought power to reinforce his
own self-esteem as well as to do good for the people, La
Guardia had hopes for a national office. As has been discussed, he thought about running for the presidency at the
head of a progressive coalition in 1940. But any national
progressive organization would have to be an effective one.
When Philip La Follette organized a new Progressive party
in 1938, La Guardia decided to remain aloof, fearing that
the party's supporters were political amateurs who could
do little for his ambitions. Besides, he preferred to see what
Roosevelt would do. Harold Ickes in 1937 mentioned La
Guardia as a possible successor to Roosevelt if the president did not choose to seek a third term. Fiorello was also
interested in a vice-presidential bid on either the Republican or Democratic tickets. As an independent Republican
who supported Roosevelt, the New Deal, and the ALP, La
Guardia was well placed to go with either party or with a
strong third party. Wendell Willkie, the 1940 Republican
presidential candidate, was interested in La Guardia as
his vice-presidential running mate. But Willkie's advisors
quashed this idea; they did not trust Fiorello's political loyalty and thought that he could embarrass the Republicans
if he publicly turned down their nomination and came out
for Roosevelt. Roosevelt thought of La Guardia as a possible vice-presidential candidate on a Democratic ticket led
by Cordell Hull (Roosevelt's secretary of state) but that
would happen only if Roosevelt decided against a third
term.

There was also discussion in political and journalistic

circles about La Guardia getting a cabinet post (secretary of war or secretary of labor) or an ambassador's position. Fiorello had some influential backers who were attempting to get a major post for him. Berle, for example, tried unsuccessfully to secure a cabinet appointment for La Guardia in 1940. Roosevelt in 1940 had thought of appointing Fiorello secretary of war or possibly making him an executive deputy who would be the liaison between the president and the governmental units involved with defense production. These ideas were rejected by Roosevelt's advisors, who felt Fiorello was too independent and not a team player.

La Guardia's failure to obtain a major national position despite his public visibility and general approval can be related to some of the same factors that made him an effective congressman and mayor. He was a showman who dramatized causes and vented his anger in public. These tactics often won a public hearing on legislation or policies he supported. However, they also made him appear too "flamboyant and . . . aggressive" to some, such as Governor Lehman. As Tugwell relates, La Guardia had the wrong style and personality for those in the administration who felt it was time "to cultivate conservatism" by de-emphasizing New Deal issues in an effort to win conservative support for Roosevelt's positions on international affairs.

Other factors conspired to keep La Guardia in New York. Roosevelt was interested in having Republicans in his cabinet in an effort to develop bipartisanship on foreign policy issues, but La Guardia did not really represent a Republican viewpoint. Also, Fiorello, as a progressive leader and potential third-party candidate, was a possible competitor for the Democrats. However, once the president decided to run for a third term, he knew that a third-party progressive organization would be ineffective. As such, nothing was to be gained by preempting that party by putting one of its leaders into the cabinet. La Guardia was even thwarted by some of his supporters and friends, who wanted to keep him as mayor because the city needed him.

La Guardia had other thoughts for higher office. He had contemplated running for the U.S. Senate in 1938 but decided against it because of his recent reelection as mayor, believing that it would be unfair to leave his post just a year after his strong victory. He also thought about trying for the governorship in 1942 rather than running again for mayor in 1941, but he doubted that he could get Republican support. The only political base he could rely on was the ALP, but that party was already on the way to a factional split that would severely weaken it. La Guardia had to satisfy himself with an appointment in August 1940 as chairman of the American section of the United States–Canadian Joint Permanent Defense Board, which was responsible for coordinating U.S.-Canadian defenses, and an appointment in May 1941 as director of the Office of Civilian Defense. Although both were presidential appointments, they were not what Fiorello had wanted.

The Office of Civilian Defense was in charge of keeping morale high, improving national security, and setting up civilian organizations for home defense. Fiorello traveled extensively around the country developing a civilian defense system. During World War II, La Guardia also tried to be appointed a brigadier general overseeing the governing of captured North African territories and subsequently Italy. Roosevelt apparently was agreeable to this appointment at first, and La Guardia was so convinced that it would be announced in 1943 that he even had a uniform made as he prepared to relinquish his mayoral duties. However, the appointment never came. According to various sources, his appointment was opposed by the military, which resented political interference in a military situation; by Secretary of War Henry L. Stimson and other political leaders, who saw La Guardia's style as a possible source of trouble for Roosevelt; and by La Guardia's fusion backers, particularly Burlingham and Seabury, who, according to Robert Moses, wanted Fiorello to remain in New York as mayor. Other instances in which Roosevelt expressed interest in bringing the mayor into the military also ended in failure.

Going for Another Term

His ambition for higher office was clearly a factor in La Guardia's reluctance to run for a third term. However, numerous supporters urged him to seek reelection. Berle, for example, told Fiorello that he should run with the expectation that Roosevelt would bring him into the cabinet before his mayoral term was over; therefore, he would not have to spend another four years as mayor. But there were problems besides La Guardia's own hesitation. Although Seabury continued to support a La Guardia-led fusion ticket, all was not well. La Guardia had disappointed many reformers, including Seabury, when in 1940 (likely at Roosevelt's behest) the mayor had appointed Jimmy Walker as an impartial labor mediator for the women's-coat-and-suit business in the city. In his eagerness to please Roosevelt and other Washington powers, Fiorello seemed to stray from his earlier independence. It also seemed that the mayor was striving to win conservative support (later he even curried favor with the Democratic bosses) in an effort to secure higher office. Furthermore, his blocked ambitions for a position outside of New York fueled his resentments, and he began to take out his hostility and unhappiness on his subordinates and friends. All these factors lost him some political backing by 1941 and after.

In addition, the City Fusion party had become politically insignificant by 1941, partly because of La Guardia's patronage neglect and his interest in the ALP. (The Progressive party was defunct by 1941). Once again, conservatives in the Republican party opposed La Guardia. The ALP organization was beginning to break apart. The left (Communist) wing of the ALP was opposed to American entry into World War II and opposed La Guardia because of his strong support for intervention. By this time a number of Communists had entered the ALP and gained control of its Manhattan branch. Although the state committee and the other borough organizations remained non-Communist, as did most of the rank and file, the movement of Communists into the ALP, as well as the divisive isolationist-interventionist issue, generated opposition to La Guardia. With problems in his Republican and ALP organizational support, La Guardia was clearly in trouble.

Yet, he had his strengths, too. Whatever the politicians thought of La Guardia, he was still a charismatic public figure who had a loyal following. And he had been an active and effective mayor. One had only to see the list of accomplishments printed on the letterhead of such groups as the Citizens Non-Partisan Movement to Draft La Guardia for Mayor to realize how much he had done. Among his notable achievements were: an honest government, new hospitals and district health centers, new highways, the air terminal (later he would begin work on a second airport), improved housing, new parks, a unified subway system, a labor policy that protected workers while treating management fairly, and a good credit rating for the city. The Democrats had been slow or deficient in providing any of these.

La Guardia's organizational support eventually fell into place either because of outside forces or primary victories. The Communist elements in the ALP changed their opposition to La Guardia's interventionism after Germany attacked Russia in June 1941. With the Soviet Union now in the war, the Communist line was to support entry for the United States as well. The ALP was now solidly in La Guardia's corner. Republican party endorsement came only after a hard-fought primary that left the party in New York badly split. Some of the borough organizations had backed

John R. Davies, who opposed La Guardia's interventionist foreign policy position and his lack of support for Republican nominees on the state and national level. Also, La Guardia, who earlier had become a member of the ALP, was a very questionable Republican. Davies, in contrast, was a leading Republican who wanted to take the party back to what he saw as its conservative roots. Yet La Guardia had the good-government issue, his persistent attacks on Tammany, and the support of such prominent Republicans as Wendell Willkie, the 1940 Republican candidate for president. Apparently on the basis of his past record, La Guardia managed to win the Republican primary, but by a much smaller margin than in his 1937 primary victory. Clearly, the opposition was building, and Fiorello would face a stiff challenge from the Democrats in 1941.

La Guardia ran on the Republican, ALP, and City Fusion tickets, as well as on that of a quickly organized United City party. This last organization was formed primarily by Berle, along with a liberal Democratic group, Affiliated Young Democrats, that sought to oust the machine bosses and put the Democratic party under liberal control. Its intentions were to give the mayor an extra line on the ballot and to appeal to Democrats who did not want to back the machine candidates. As before, La Guardia's support came from two main sources: (a) progressives and good-government advocates who did not care which party label he wore, and (b) ethnic voters, particularly those from the more recent immigrant groups. La Guardia faced his toughest contest in 1941 because the Democrats finally began to understand Fiorello's reform and ethnic appeal and picked a candidate who they hoped could offer a somewhat similar attraction.

William O'Dwyer, the Brooklyn district attorney, was the Democratic choice in 1941. O'Dwyer had an excellent reputation as a hard-working government official who had brought some notorious criminals to justice in Brooklyn.

He was also not associated with Tammany and was connected instead with the Brooklyn machine. Although Irish, and therefore part of that older and politically powerful ethnic group, O'Dwyer was to make a strong appeal to the newer groups as well. Once again, ethnic issues loomed large in the campaign.

Ethnic Wars

From 1938 to 1941, New York City experienced a significant increase in anti-Semitic activity as the approach and outbreak of World War II intensified ethnic tensions. Not only was the German-American Bund still meeting, but in 1938 the largely Irish-Catholic Christian Front, an outgrowth of Father Charles Coughlin's National Union for Social Justice movement, emerged in the city. Coughlin, a demagogue who made skillful use of the radio, parroted Nazi anti-Semitic rhetoric and drew a large following among those who looked for scapegoats and simplistic explanations for the troubles of the times. The Front was a product of these factors as well as of the tensions over ethnic succession. The Christian Front led a wave of anti-Semitic terror, including street meetings, boycotts of Jewish merchants, and attacks on Jewish people, in Jewish communities in the South Bronx, Washington Heights in northern Manhattan, Flatbush in Brooklyn, and elsewhere in the city. The Christian Front also was involved in 1940 in a bizarre plot (foiled by the FBI) to inspire an anti-Semitic movement in America and overthrow the United States government. An even more violent version of the Front emerged in the Christian Mobilizers, and numerous acts of vandalism and violence continued into the war years against synagogues, Jewish-owned stores, and Jewish New Yorkers.

Naturally, then, anti-Semitism and the Front became major issues in the 1941 mayoral campaign. Fearing that what was happening in Germany could take place in America, the Jewish community wanted La Guardia to take action to eliminate the anti-Semitic threats and acts. The mayor, although a consistent champion of free speech, always sought to protect the public safety and avoid violence. He urged the police and courts to take action if anti-Semites violated a city law that made the abuse of racial and ethnic groups illegal. He also had undercover agents investigate anti-Semitic groups and report on their activities. Arrests of anti-Semitic street-corner agitators increased, but there was no decrease in meetings. The Front and other anti-Semitic and pro-Nazi elements were also isolationists who opposed any American involvement in the coming war. Therefore, antiwar meetings at times included anti-Jewish rhetoric and anti-Semitic groups. As with the 1937 Bund parade, the mayor was caught between his beliefs in the constitutional rights of free speech and assembly and the right of abused minorities to seek redress. As the arrests of the agitators increased, La Guardia commented that New York will be open as always to free speech "but the authorities will deal properly with any misguided troublemakers who, under the guise of free speech, slander or vilify peaceful groups residing in the city." The police also arrested anyone who interfered with the speakers, further antagonizing those who wanted the pro-Nazi elements off the streets.

William O'Dwyer, the Democratic candidate in 1941, wasted little time in bringing the anti-Semitic issue into the campaign. He suggested that the mayor had been either ineffective or unwilling to deal with anti-Semites. He accused the mayor of bringing anti-Catholics (such as Fama) and anti-Semites into positions in his administration. O'Dwyer asserted that as Brooklyn district attorney, he had not allowed anti-Semitic agitators on that borough's streets and that, if elected, he would get the Front off the streets of the rest of the city. The issue threatened to hurt the mayor. One letter sent to him by a Jewish supporter noted that "we cannot understand why you permit a small group of hatemongers to hold street meetings and preach the doctrine of race and religious hatred."

Once the issue was raised, however, La Guardia was able to manipulate it to his advantage. Like others before him, O'Dwyer had played to the mayor's strength by introducing the ethnic factor in the campaign. La Guardia, utilizing his appointees and supporters, set out to label the Irish O'Dwyer as an anti-Semite and to challenge his boasts that he kept his borough's streets free of anti-Semites. La Guardia accused O'Dwyer of accepting support from anti-Jewish groups and even of being the candidate of the pro-Nazi element. According to O'Dwyer, rumors were spread that he was anti-Semitic and belonged to the Front. Both were false.

Although O'Dwyer tried to refute charges of anti-Semitism, he clearly was in a weaker position on this issue than the mayor. The Front was predominately Irish; and therefore O'Dwyer, who was Irish, was suspect. In fact, O'Dwyer had fought against the Front and advocated tolerance on many occasions. In his speech accepting the nomination, he had lambasted the city's anti-Semitic elements and promised a continued effort to eliminate them. O'Dwyer conjectured years later that La Guardia had gained Jewish votes by railing against the Front, but saved some Catholic votes by not eliminating it. As the Democratic candidate later noted, La Guardia "could always shake his fist at Hitler, or say something dramatic, and hold onto the Jews, who in the main were not alert to what La Guardia was doing to them with the Christian Front." Yet, given his long commitment to fighting anti-Semitism and his concern for public safety, the mayor surely was committed to ending the anti-Semitic terror in the city. Every indication is that La Guardia worked to stop the anti-Jewish attacks including, as anti-Semitic violence peaked in the

1940s, setting up a special detective unit in 1943 to report on and take action against anti-Semitic agitators.

O'Dwyer eventually came to understand the mayor's ability to exploit ethnic issues. La Guardia's own beliefs on tolerance, his ability to dramatize situations, and his political instincts and hard-hitting tactics were difficult to beat. As one usually Democratic Jewish newspaper commented when it came out for Fiorello, "the Jewish population knows that they always have in him a trustworthy, devoted big brother." La Guardia's image as protector of the downtrodden and abused was not a new image for the mayor, and one he believed in as well as enjoyed and effectively utilized.

The Democrats made other attempts to inject the issue of anti-Semitism into the campaign, particularly after La Guardia criticized Governor Lehman, the leading Jewish politician in the state. Although this too may have influenced votes, it also brought criticism from some in the Jewish community who objected (in vain) to the use of ethnic appeals in the election contest.

The War in Europe and the 1941 Campaign

Although mayors have nothing to do with deciding foreign policy, the interventionist-isolationist arguments became a part of the mayoral campaign rhetoric in New York City. America's reaction to the policies of Nazi Germany was important to Jewish New Yorkers, who endorsed politicians who opposed those policies and backed intervention in the war. O'Dwyer, like La Guardia, supported Roosevelt's foreign policy, but the mayor had a long commitment to the anti-Nazi position and was clearly identified in the public mind with intervention. He was honorary chairman of the New York chapter of the Committee to Defend America by Aiding the Allies, a leading interventionist organization, and called for full scale aid to Great Britain. He noted as well that "we American people would gladly and voluntarily stand with England now rather than be compelled to negotiate later with Hitler." He stated that "we will not accept a Hitler-dominated world." He had endorsed many times the idea of more American aid to those fighting the Axis.

In his support for intervention the mayor broke with some of his progressive allies, such as Wheeler and Philip La Follette, who were strong isolationists. La Guardia had always been more attuned than the western progressives to the world outside the United States. To the public there was also a connection between La Guardia and Roosevelt that went back to 1932, when Fiorello had led the effort to push the New Deal program through Congress. Roosevelt's public support for La Guardia in 1941 confirmed this tie. For the isolationist New Yorker, O'Dwyer could easily appear to be the lesser of two evils. According to a 1941 public opinion survey, this issue affected the election and cost the mayor some isolationist votes.

A Part-Time Mayor: The 1941 Campaign

There were other issues as well. The Democrats claimed, with some accuracy, that La Guardia was a part-time mayor, that his civilian defense job often kept him out of the city and left him with insufficient time for city problems. The Democrats also accused Fiorello of having appointed Communists in his administration, and it was implied that he was one himself—a charge with no substance. That this issue was raised at all was mainly because of Stanley Isaacs' (the Republican-Fusion borough president of Manhattan) appointment in 1937 of Simon Gerson, a Communist, to his staff. Paul Kern, the mayor's civil service commission chairman, supported this appointment, and was suspected himself of ties to possibly Communist organizations. However, the mayor apparently disposed of the issue by refusing to endorse Isaacs for renomination in 1941. Kern, due to this factor and others, was fired in 1942. Fiorello was not an ideologue. He had fought Marxists of various varieties throughout his entire career and he did not welcome Communist support. Yet the "red" label was always damaging to a politician, and the Democrats tried to make the most of this phony issue. O'Dwyer also tried to picture himself as the New Deal candidate, a tactic that failed after Roosevelt publicly and strongly endorsed La Guardia. As FDR said, "Mayor La Guardia and his administration have given to the city the most honest and, I believe, the most efficient municipal government of any within my recollection."

Analyzing the Vote

The war in Europe and the debate in the United States over intervention versus isolation took votes away from La Guardia. In addition, the mayor's own failings, particularly his growing inattention to the job as he took on national duties, diluted his support. He won, but by the narrowest margin in a mayoral race in over thirty years, with just over 52 percent of the vote, as compared with 60.1 percent in 1937. His vote among New York's ethnic groups illustrates the impact of the various issues.

La Guardia's vote in Irish and German election districts declined from 1937. He received 36.8 percent of the Irish vote in 1937, but only 23.9 percent in 1941. His German vote declined from 46.4 percent in 1937 to 28.3 percent in 1941. The Irish and German votes reflected their responses to the foreign policy issue (both ethnic groups tended to be isolationist), and to their sense that La Guardia did not represent their interests.

Jewish voters, as before, gave La Guardia strong support, with 72.8 percent of their vote. They rallied to Fiorello on the basis of his good-government, liberal, and anti-Nazi policies. In fact, it was the Jewish vote that secured the election for La Guardia.

The black voter, if the predominately black Twenty-first Assembly District in Harlem is any gauge, also strongly supported the mayor. He won 71.2 percent of the vote in this district.

Oddly, the other ethnic group that had been a solid part of his base and for which he had spoken over the years indicated a break with the mayor. The Italian election districts, which had given Fiorello 62.6 percent of their vote in 1937, provided only 46.1 percent in 1941. This decline resulted from a number of factors. At the time of Fiorello's entry into politics and continuing into 1933, when he was first elected mayor, the Democratic party had not yet strongly responded to Italian desires for political recognition. The Democratic politicians, as already noted, began to understand these needs in light of La Guardia's victories and began to fulfill them, although slowly, and thereby eventually picked up some votes. By 1941, there was even some sentiment in the Italian community that La Guardia had neglected this group and could have provided more appointments. The impact of the depression over the years, La Guardia's public criticism of Mussolini in 1940, and his strong ties to Roosevelt and an interventionist foreign policy also affected the downward turn of this vote. The Italian community tended to be isolationist and deeply worried about an American war with Italy; many therefore did not support the mayor's calls for more American involvement in the war. Furthermore, when Italy invaded France and entered World War II in June 1940, Roosevelt had angrily remarked that "the hand that held the dagger has struck it into the back of its neighbor." Italian-Americans considered this "stab-in-the-back" statement an ethnic slur, and it apparently cost Roosevelt some votes. The president's endorsement of La Guardia in 1941 therefore did not help him with Italian voters.

La Guardia, however, had won three mayoral campaigns because of his support among the new immigrant groups. His victories were based mainly on Italian votes in 1933, Italian and Jewish votes in 1937, Jewish votes in 1941, and black votes in all three elections. Appealing to the aspirations of various groups was a well-used campaign tactic in New York politics. In a city where ethnic groups were also interest groups, and rivalries were intense and prolonged, politicians often rose to power on the basis of tribal appeals. La Guardia therefore was not unique in his use of these tactics. However, he was better at it than other politicians and emerged at a time when the politically upwardly mobile new-immigrant voters needed a leader and protector. Italians in particular wanted political positions and acknowledgment as an important element in the city's ethnic hierarchy. Jews were especially interested in making other Americans comprehend the Nazi danger and speak out against it. During many of his mayoral years, La Guardia became the personification of both groups' desires. Yet, the ethnic appeal, used not only in congressional and mayoral campaigns but also in gubernatorial and presidential elections of this era, could be a damaging tactic. Appealing to some groups at the expense of others, exploiting foreign-policy issues to divide groups, and using accusations of intolerance as a political tactic to smear opponents were not good for the city. The campaigns of this period clearly contributed to the ethnic fears, tensions, and conflicts that emerged. Victorious politicians were sometimes left with a divided and suspicious constituency, which made it difficult for them to govern effectively.

A Too-Busy Mayor

La Guardia's third election victory was unprecedented for a New York reform mayor. Although it is generally acknowledged that Fiorello's last term was his least effective, compared to his predecessors he continued to offer good government to New York. The main problem in his third term was the one raised in the election—that his other duties and interests took him away from his mayoral job. From Tuesday through Thursday of each week, La Guardia was in Washington, D.C., in his position as civilian defense director. He would then come back to New York for a few days to deal with city issues. While La Guardia was away, Newbold Morris, the Fusion city council president, would administer the city government. The constant travel back and forth to Washington, his attendance at cabinet meetings in his capacity as director of the Office of Civilian Defense, and his positions as president of the U.S. Conference of Mayors and chairman of the American section of the U.S.-Canadian Joint Permanent Defense Board took their toll on his time.

La Guardia's codirector of the Office of Civilian Defense was Eleanor Roosevelt, who began her work in September, 1941. Having the president's wife, who was well known and respected in her own right, as codirector, added status and recognition to the Office of Civilian Defense and to La Guardia. But civilian defense director was not the job the mayor had desired; he had hoped for a high position with wide powers and a large staff. Seeking status and an outlet for his ambition, La Guardia tried to make the civilian defense position more than it was. Traveling around the country making speeches and planning for a wartime emergency kept Fiorello in the newspapers but not at the center of power. Although he was dissatisfied, he was reluctant to give the position up because it allowed him to attend cabinet meetings and brought him some national recognition. Eventually, however, La Guardia's independence, his need to dramatize what he was doing, his desire for more authority, and his sometimes abrasive management style led Roosevelt to pressure La Guardia to resign in February 1942. Another factor was that by 1942 the country was at war and needed a full-time civilian defense director. As the *New York Times* commented in an editorial on January 3, 1942:

> The whole trouble with the present arrangement is that two great full-time jobs are being handled on part time. . . . We simply believe . . . that on December 7 the Office of Civilian Defense and the office of Mayor of New York ceased suddenly, definitely and irrevocably to be two offices that could be filled competently by a single man. The sooner Mr. La Guardia recognizes this incontestable fact, the sooner will his equanimity be equal to the demands now made upon it and the sooner will his great ability be put to the best service of his city and his country.

La Guardia simply could not do both jobs. Even before the Pearl Harbor attack, his inability to handle both posts was demonstrated by foul-ups in the Office of Civilian Defense and by his overall lack of planning. Eleanor Roosevelt also resigned from the agency, and James M. Landis, a Harvard Law School dean who had been appointed in January 1942 to serve as executive officer under the mayor's supervision, became the director.

As usual, La Guardia had believed he could do it all, but there were limits to even his energy. World War II made governing New York harder as increasing numbers of capable city officials and civil service workers went into the armed forces, the federal service, or defense work. Burgeoning city problems and his disappointment with not securing an important national position increased the ambitious mayor's irritability and frustration. During the time he served as both mayor and civilian defense director, La Guardia clearly was overworked, and this, along with his unhappiness over a blocked career, led him to neglect city matters and make foolish and intemperate decisions. For example, he interfered in the workings of the markets department and appointed individuals who had helped him in the campaign, something he was loath to do earlier in his administration. This resulted in the resignation of an effective commissioner of markets, William Fellowes Morgan, in late 1941. The mayor got into a dispute with Paul Kern, Civil Service Commission chairman, over allowing some individuals with ties to Boss Flynn to bypass the merit system. Kern and his commission were suspended in early February 1942, but not without a blast from Kern regarding the mayor's inattention to city concerns, his temper, and his political wheeling and dealing in an effort to secure higher office.

The publicity surrounding Fiorello's actions tarnished his reputation and indicated that, as Morgan noted, he was too involved with his other work to resolve problems or even meet with his department heads. La Guardia's ambition now sometimes seemed to obscure his vision of good government and reform. But one must put this in context; Fiorello was still far superior to the Tammany bosses and previous mayors, and even at this point he ran an exemplary administration.

There were other problems. As the mayor's years in office wore on, the city began spending too much and balancing the budget became more difficult. Even high taxes did not make up for La Guardia's expenditures. Therefore, La Guardia was forced to make more use of bonds, which would carry the fiscal deficiencies into future decades. This was a fiscal approach that he had opposed in the early stages of his administration. Criticism of the mayor's fiscal policies mounted. Although some city services could have been more cost efficient, New York received a lot in return for this long-term debt. A concerned government offering numerous services to its people cost money. La Guardia, if not always the people of New York, understood this simple fact. The mayor was still bent on creating a better more livable New York.

He also was still very much the politician, and he avoided certain actions that would be unpopular with voters, such as raising the five-cent subway fare, even though this would have allowed the city to improve the train system and make it economically sound. He also avoided making changes in pension policies, although defects in the city's pension system forced New York into long-term and substantial pension payments, conceivably to the detriment of the city's daily fiscal needs. The financial problems that emerged for New York in later decades could be said to have begun with La Guardia. But it would have taken a particularly prescient individual to foresee that the federal government would cut back its help after the war and that the city would eventually face bankruptcy. Fiorello gave New Yorkers a government dedicated to their well-being and urban amenities not found elsewhere in the country. Although La Guardia was aware of growing fiscal problems and decline in the city during the war, he could easily attribute these to the wartime withdrawal of federal funds. The cost of the war effort had a detrimental effect on many city budgets. The mayor was anticipating that after the war a generous federal government would once again pick up the funding slack, as it had during the depression. That this did not happen, and that the city's problems worsened, was less the result of Fiorello's lack of ability or vision and more the consequence of a national government that did not always understand its fiscal responsibilities to America's cities.

On the Radio

Although it is clear that La Guardia's popularity declined in his last term, he still remained a favorite with many New Yorkers and certainly stayed in the public eye. Beginning in January 1942, Fiorello took to the radio with a popular weekly program broadcast from City Hall on Sunday afternoons. He spoke on various topics, discussing everything from world events to how to save money on food to the obligations of landlords to their tenants to issues concerning his family. He warned individuals who cheated the public that they would be punished, informed people of their rights, and discussed rationing requirements. During a newspaper deliverers' strike in July 1945, he even read the Sunday comics over the air so that the children of the city would not have to miss the comic pages of the paper. Acting out each character while reading Dick Tracy and adding moral lessons on why a life of crime did not pay, La Guardia brought the comic pages to life for New Yorkers. Although such a radio program might seem bizarre to some people, it suited La Guardia perfectly to be the center of attention and the leader taking care of his children—the people of New York. Ever since his youth, Fiorello had craved respect and status and enjoyed providing for, admonishing, and directing his flock. It was probably one of the reasons that he found it so difficult to accept criticism, which he considered a betrayal by those for whom he had worked so long and hard. Criticism kept coming nonetheless, particularly of his handling of issues of race and ethnicity.

Racial Tensions

Although the mayor still had much difficulty with anti-Semitic vandalism in the city after the 1941 election, the major ethnic problem for his third administration was the second Harlem riot in 1943. Conditions in the black community had improved after the 1935 riot, mainly because of La Guardia's efforts to aid this group and the New Deal's work to improve the economy. He had support from blacks because he provided new schools and housing in their neighborhoods, brought them into his administration, and attacked discrimination in housing, civil service, and the city bureaucracy.

La Guardia also played an important role in getting Roosevelt to issue Executive Order 8802, which created the Fair Employment Practices Committee (FEPC), in June

1941. The FEPC, set up to deal with employment discrimination in government agencies and in companies involved in defense work, resulted mainly from the efforts of A. Philip Randolph and his March on Washington movement. Randolph, president of the Brotherhood of Sleeping Car Porters and an important black leader, and Walter White, the NAACP executive director, suggested to Roosevelt that La Guardia would be a good first chairman of the FEPC. Hesitant about having created the FEPC, the president picked another individual as chairman instead, someone with more temperate views. Nevertheless, the fact that Fiorello was suggested by major black leaders indicated that they trusted him and accepted his views on racial tolerance. The mayor strongly supported FEPC goals and later served on a committee to try to set up a permanent postwar FEPC.

In New York City, even before the FEPC was created, the mayor took action against employment discrimination in companies that did business with government. He went after employment agencies (over which he had some control because they were licensed by the city) that would not identify those government-related companies that made discriminatory hiring requests. He tried to take away the offending agencies' licenses but was initially prevented from doing so by the courts. Later he pressured agencies to reject discriminatory requests and in 1942 secured a city ordinance that forced agencies to keep records of discriminatory employment requests and allow the license department to see the records. If an agency refused, it could lose its license. However, if an employer insisted on running an ad specifying, for example, racial preferences, there was little the mayor or the city would or could do.

Fiorello initially was reluctant to use government power against a private company. But he hoped that once identified, the discriminating employer would bend to moral pressure and eliminate the practice. Once again, following in the footsteps of the muckraking progressives, La Guardia felt that once an immoral action was revealed to the public, the resultant moral outrage would rectify the problem. If any criticism can be made of La Guardia in regard to employment discrimination, it is that he put too much emphasis on the ability of moral principles, education, and faith in democracy to eliminate prejudice and change stereotypic views. Instead, as others such as Marcantonio contended at that time, tougher antidiscrimination laws were needed. Fiorello eventually and hesitantly came to support legislation barring employment discrimination in private companies that had city work contracts. Although La Guardia used legislation and government authority to counteract discrimination, he preferred a gradual process that would not force better intergroup relations and thereby cause friction. Although a gradualist, La Guardia still worked fervently to open up jobs to all and to support tolerance in the city.

Yet, many problems of racial discrimination remained. Police brutality against blacks was still an issue, as was discrimination against the hiring of black professors in the city colleges, the closing by police of the popular Savoy ballroom in Harlem, where interracial dancing occurred, and discrimination against blacks in housing. This last issue was one in which the mayor was strongly involved, and in a way that was surprising, considering his past record. La Guardia had been solidly against racial discrimination in housing and was influential in getting various housing projects integrated during the 1930s and 1940s. In April 1943 the city announced a new housing complex, called Stuyvesant Town, which would be developed with the cooperation of private enterprise and government as part of a long-term effort to construct decent low- and middle-income housing that would be needed in the postwar period. The Metropolitan Life Insurance Company, working with the city, built Stuyvesant Town in lower Manhattan as part of the city's attempt to interest insurance companies and savings banks in slum clearance projects. New York would offer tax breaks, city-owned land, and the use of eminent domain to acquire additional property necessary for this thirty-five-building apartment project.

Robert Moses, the city's parks commissioner and housing advisor, had actually negotiated the contract for the complex, but La Guardia, as mayor, was also involved. The problem was not the construction or land for the housing, but rather the tenant-selection process. Metropolitan, which had been involved in discriminatory housing policies before, stated that no blacks would be allowed as tenants. Claiming a desire to safeguard their investment and protect property values as rationales for their racism, the company stood firm on their right to select tenants.

As a private citizen or congressman, La Guardia would have responded quickly and adamantly against the company's policy. As mayor he hesitated, which brought opposition from many of his long-time supporters, who did not understand his reluctance to move on a clear case of racial discrimination. La Guardia had not become a racist. He was faced with a dilemma similar to that faced by many black leaders later on in the urban renewal years of the 1950s and 1960s: the choice was either to accept segregated housing projects or have no housing built at all. In this case, La Guardia's choices were either to accept the contract with company-controlled tenant selection or risk alienating this and other private companies that were interested in constructing needed housing. If Metropolitan decided not to build, what would the impact be on private enterprise involvement in postwar slum clearance and housing? The mayor was urged to eliminate the racism or to drop the idea for Stuyvesant Town. La Guardia decided to accept Metropolitan Life's contract for Stuyvesant Town and was severely criticized for his decision, even by old friends such as Walter White.

Fiorello's decision was based on a number of considerations. He had long supported better housing in the city. He
also had a good working relationship with Robert Moses,
who had been very successful with public works projects in
New York. Moses was influential in convincing the mayor
of the need for private money in public housing construction, and of the necessity of getting and keeping Metropolitan involved in the project. Moses had offered no opposition to the company's insistence on controlling tenant
selection. The mayor, still wearing too many hats during
this wartime period, was not fully cognizant of the implica-
tions of Metropolitan's tenant policies at first. He was then
reluctant to interfere and perhaps prevent the entry of private enterprise funds into slum clearance and housing.
Moses urged La Guardia to do nothing to upset the agreement. As such, Fiorello decided not to take direct action.
He hoped instead that a court judgment would be made
against the discriminatory policy that would then give him
the legal means to open up Stuyvesant Town to blacks.
However, this response was not an adequate one and did
nothing to lift the racial restrictions. Although immediately
prior to signing the contract on August 4, 1943, the mayor
had stated he would fight with legal means any discrimination at Stuyvesant Town, this was too little, too late.

The controversy over this housing project and the increasing racial friction in the city convinced La Guardia not
to make the same mistake again and also to make amends
to the black community. He secured in 1944 an agreement
with Metropolitan to build the Riverton housing project in
Harlem. Already involved in a court case over discrimination in Stuyvesant Town, Metropolitan was willing to build
such housing in an effort to prove that it was not a racist
company. Unfortunately, the courts never provided La
Guardia with the means to challenge Metropolitan's discriminatory racial policies. The state courts later ruled in a
case brought by the NAACP that Metropolitan could con-

trol tenant selection in any way it wanted. However, in 1944 the city council passed a bill, which the mayor supported because it did not threaten the Stuyvesant Town project, that prevented racist tenant selection in future housing constructed under joint private enterprise-government co-operation. This legislation laid the framework for future policies of open tenant selection. Stuyvesant Town itself was not integrated until 1951, by new city legislation. Thus, some good eventually came out of the protests against Stuyvesant Town discrimination.

The Second Harlem Riot

Racial tensions ran high in New York City. A major race riot erupted in Harlem in August 1943, a few months after the plans for Stuyvesant Town were announced. Race riots had already occurred in Detroit and other cities prior to the August 1 New York riot. The mayor was therefore well aware of escalating racial tensions in the nation and was able to prepare somewhat for these problems in New York. He worked with white and black leaders to analyze the riot in Detroit and try to prevent one in New York through new policy announcements. The police demonstrated a willing-ness to hire more blacks for the force, and the city devel-oped plans for new housing in Harlem. Yet, the mayor probably helped increase the tensions as well. Clearly the continuing animosity generated by Stuyvesant Town was not beneficial, and La Guardia should have taken a quicker, more forceful stand against discrimination in the complex. Yet, he waited until August 4 (the day the contract was signed) to state publicly what he had earlier determined, that he hoped the courts would rule against the discrimi-natory policy so that he could take action against it. A state-ment days earlier might have helped to calm tensions, but the mayor said nothing, lest he ruin the housing deal.

    The two-day riot began when rumors spread throughout

Harlem that a white police officer had shot and killed a black serviceman. In fact, a black soldier had been slightly wounded in an altercation involving the police and a woman the soldier and others were trying to release from arrest. The rumors prevailed, however, and looting, vandalism, and arson erupted, resulting in 6 people being killed and 185 injured. Once this riot was quelled, the mayor made efforts to avoid future ones. He went on the radio during the riot to try to calm the situation, and afterward he delivered a number of broadcasts urging tolerance and racial harmony. The school system began a course for teachers that described the contributions blacks had made to American life and emphasized democracy and tolerance. The schools also developed new programs to enhance black pride. In addition, the mayor stated his intentions to develop new housing in black neighborhoods in Manhattan, Brooklyn, Queens, and the Bronx.

Of major concern to the black community was the inflated prices they were paying for food, rent, and other necessities in their neighborhoods. These high prices often violated the regulations of the federal Office of Price Administration (OPA). La Guardia quickly secured the federal government's promise to place an OPA office in Harlem and to hire blacks for important positions in the agency. Within a few months, the city also saw the implementation of a federal rent-control policy. Not only did the OPA make more of an effort to deal with high prices but the city's markets department also began a thorough monitoring of Harlem prices and found numerous violations. La Guardia decided toward the end of the year to establish the Mayor's Committee on Unity to research and prevent discrimination and racial intolerance. Always a believer in education as the way to improve race relations, La Guardia saw the committee's work as providing the data to smooth intergroup relations and avert future riots. Finally, La Guardia reopened the Savoy ballroom, which had been closed before the riot, ostensibly because of vice and health concerns. Harlem leaders, however, felt the real reason for revoking the ballroom's license was racial prejudice provoked by interracial mixing. The mayor had accepted the reports of city and military officials recommending the closing at face value. The riot caused him to have second thoughts about the Savoy, and in an effort to remove an issue of contention, he allowed the ballroom to open its doors again.

All of La Guardia's postriot actions were commendable and indicated his commitment to supporting tolerance. Yet many of them could have occurred earlier, which perhaps would have averted a riot. High prices, lack of housing, the Stuyvesant Town controversy, and intercultural educational efforts in the schools all could have received more attention earlier. In some cases, La Guardia's heavy work load in too many jobs prevented him from attending to the details of the mayor's office and the city, and he therefore was not always aware of conditions. In other cases, as with the Mayor's Committee on Unity, La Guardia waited too long to create such a body. He did not like official committees that functioned outside the usual governmental framework and were thus removed from his control.

It also could be argued that La Guardia should have taken more action after the riot. Such problems as employment discrimination, OPA violations, and antiblack vandalism (in apartment houses and neighborhoods where blacks were moving) persisted. Perhaps any mayor could only do so much in a country where racism was prevalent. The war was also a factor. Surely World War II shortages limited La Guardia's efforts to build housing and new schools in black areas. And black anger and frustration at the idea of fighting for democracy and tolerance abroad while facing segregation in the army and in American society in general were issues beyond La Guardia's control. Nonetheless, quicker action and increased attention from the mayor would have helped to ease the racial frustrations and tensions.

The Ethnic Politician

Probably no individual could have calmed the ethnic and racial tensions of the 1930s and 1940s, which were exacerbated by such factors as the depression, ethnic succession, nazism, Coughlin-inspired anti-Semitism, and World War II. At times, as with the Harlem riots, La Guardia did much to ameliorate the hostility and frustration of the involved community. Yet, clearly, as in the Stuyvesant Town decision, he at times stirred up ethnic anger. Like many Americans, La Guardia also got caught up in wartime hysteria. During the war he supported the incarceration of Japanese-Americans (most of whom were citizens) and objected to the resettling in New York of any of those released in 1944. La Guardia rationalized his intolerance and over-reacting patriotism by citing concerns about subversive activity and about public safety because of possible clashes between Japanese-Americans and other groups in New York. Yet he had no such worries about Italian or German aliens and defended their rights. Government officials had assured him that the Japanese-Americans had been thoroughly investigated and offered absolutely no subversive threat; furthermore, some Japanese-Americans had already been resettled in New York and had caused no problems. However, the mayor remained adamant in his opposition to this group. It is difficult to explain Fiorello's retreat from his lifelong belief in civil liberties and racial equity. If it was not simply war hysteria, then perhaps it was partly because of political considerations, as with the Irish. He remained intensely ambitious, and he may have feared that any defense of the Japanese-Americans would hurt his career. Although he was usually sensitive to racial and ethnic concerns and generally stood above his generation on minority issues, La Guardia was capable of serious lapses in judgment based on political or other considerations.

Also, La Guardia's close connection with Italian and Jewish political aspirations as spokesman for and protector of these groups in their New York-based struggles for recognition put him at the forefront of the challenge to Irish political power and cultural values. The mayor became the symbolic political leader of the inevitable ethnic succession taking place. Given his background, it was natural for Fiorello to assume this role. Yet, by opening up political positions to newer ethnic groups, and by using ethnic appeals in his campaigns (as did his opponents), he antagonized Irish and some German New Yorkers and increased those groups' conflict with, in particular, the Jews. La Guardia's role in the new immigrant groups' struggle for recognition should not necessarily be criticized (except in such easily resolvable cases as those of Fama and Kress) but rather simply noted as part of the ongoing ethnic competition and conflict of the time. And, of course, La Guardia was usually not the first to introduce ethnic issues into campaigns. To stay in power, to beat Tammany (which had used the ethnic concerns well), Fiorello had to fight back with similar tactics. This was the price, he believed, for providing New York with good-government reform and the new immigrant groups with ethnic representation.

Still a Reformer

The last part of his third term found La Guardia offering new reform ideas and still hoping for the emergence of an effective national Progressive party. In 1943 he began plans to institute a citywide health insurance program that would cover workers who earned no more than $5,000 per year. The plan, a voluntary one, would provide medical, hospital, and surgical insurance for workers and their families. The plan's cost would be divided between employer and employee. Reminiscent of early progressive calls for health insurance (e. g., the Progressive party's plank on this issue in 1912), the Health Insurance Plan of Greater New York (HIP) was a major step forward in providing decent and affordable health care for New Yorkers long before such programs as Medicare or Medicaid were developed. Although HIP did not go into effect until March 1947, under the next mayor, it was La Guardia's idea and one that once again linked the early progressives to the 1940s mayor. Reform and the development of a more responsive government continued to concern La Guardia.

There was some discussion in 1943 among ALP state leaders about expanding the party beyond New York. They thought in terms of developing a nationwide third party in case the Democrats or Republicans reverted to their past and chose candidates in 1944 who were not in tune with New Deal domestic and foreign policy. La Guardia supported such a move; he wanted to make sure that the New Deal accomplishments would endure. Although nothing happened—the ALP was too factionalized by this time— La Guardia continued to advocate a strong national Progressive party.

A Fourth Term?

Towards the end of his third term, La Guardia was undecided about whether he would seek reelection. Many thought that he would try for a fourth term. Fiorello might have been interested, but the still-popular mayor did not find much organizational support for another term; he had alienated too many politicians in various parties over the years to win approval for another nomination. Although La Guardia still had some support among Republicans, the leadership of the party, long disgusted with the mayor's independence and his lack of patronage offerings, decided not to back him. The general sense that Fiorello's third term had not been as effective as the first two, and the various disputes in which he had been involved, gave the Republican leaders the rationale and the political strength to distance themselves from him. The Democrats certainly would not nominate the mayor; instead they again went with O'Dwyer, who had done well in 1941.

The American Labor party, Fiorello's crucial base of support in 1937 and 1941, along with the Republicans, split into two parties by the 1945 election. The right wing of the ALP, dominated by International Ladies Garment Workers Union (ILGWU) president David Dubinsky, and Hatters, Cap, and Millinery Workers Union chief Alex Rose, had broken away in 1944 to form the Liberal party under Rose's leadership. The remaining left-wing element in the ALP, which was controlled by Communists, maintained the ALP label. The Liberal party was hostile to the mayor for a number of reasons. La Guardia had been caught in the middle of the factional dispute in the ALP. Fervently trying to prevent a split, which might hurt Roosevelt in his 1944 campaign, Fiorello in 1944 had attempted to work out a compromise that would keep the party united. The right-wing leaders, who felt that La Guardia should have supported only them and that a continued working relationship with the left wing was unfeasible, were angered by the mayor's attempt at compromise. They claimed that the mayor's actions had actually aided the left wing by muddling the differences between the two factions. Also, the mayor's temper betrayed him, and he launched some ill-advised attacks on the Liberal party leaders. Finally, La Guardia had supported ALP left-wing leader Marcantonio in his bids for Congress. Although he disagreed with some of the policies of his long-time friend and protégé, Fiorello, probably out of loyalty, continued to back him. This endorsement drew the ire of the ALP right wing. In 1945, the ALP (now containing only the left wing) backed La Guardia for a fourth term, based presumably on his efforts to keep the party strong and united, but the Liberal party did not. A nomination from only the ALP would not be enough to win an election.

Any try at a fusion ticket for the mayor was doomed—the political support was no longer there. Even some good-government people were now hostile to La Guardia, feeling that his third term had not been as satisfactory as his first two. La Guardia had incurred the wrath of good-government elements in his disputes with the Civil Service Commission in 1942 regarding the merit system and the Board of Education in 1943 regarding appointments. His temper and sometimes dictatorial methods, increasingly in evidence in his third term, had brought an open break with some of his former supporters by late 1943 and early 1944. And as noted, during Fiorello's third term his spending policies were under attack from those who felt he was not fiscally prudent and was creating an unmanageable future deficit. Although he still had Seabury's support, as well as that of other reformers who had remained loyal over the years, it was not enough. And even some of these supporters based their endorsement more on La Guardia's voter appeal than on their satisfaction with his third term.

Probably because he did not find the political organizational backing he needed, although he still was popular with many voters, La Guardia announced in May 1945 that he would not run. Enumerating the gains his three administrations had achieved for the city and claiming he could still win even if he did not get any party support, he quoted Al Smith in his May 6, 1945, address to the city, boasting that "I can run on a laundry ticket and beat these political bums any time." He went on to say that he could "lick any combination of political parties." But the mayor said he was bowing out because he had been in the office too long. And as he often did, Fiorello spoke on a personal basis to his listeners, this time asking for help in finding a house. "So I hope you will all help us find a house because it would be terrible to have to stay in office because we could not find a house to live in, wouldn't it?" He may also have decided against a fourth term because of concern about his health, which, according to Newbold Morris, was already deteriorating.

The 1945 Election and the No Deal Party

With La Guardia's removal from the campaign, the door was opened for a possible return of the Democratic machine. O'Dwyer became the nominee of the Democratic party and the ALP. The Republicans joined with the Liberal party and the City Fusion party to nominate Jonah J. Goldstein, a judge on the general sessions court and a Democrat associated with Tammany who was first appointed to the courts by Mayor Walker. Goldstein was considered a good choice by these parties because he could appeal to the large Jewish vote. Although he was an honest judge, his ties to Tammany concerned many of the good-government people, as did his earlier attempt to win the 1945 Democratic nomination. Seabury was particularly incensed and angrily stated that he would not support Goldstein. "I shall not support the sham Fusion ticket nominated by the Republican party. We now have two Tammany Hall tickets in the field."

Seabury's and other reformers' dissatisfaction resulted in an effort to put a new party in the field. Newbold Morris broke with the Republican-Liberal-City Fusion ticket (on which he had agreed to run as the candidate for city council president) after Goldstein was nominated. He then formed an independent party known as the No Deal party. La Guardia played a leading role in the development of this new political organization, claiming that he supported the party because O'Dwyer and Goldstein were unacceptable and that Morris could pull off a victory. Others suggested different reasons for his support. He might have wanted revenge on the Republicans and Liberals because of their hostility to him and therefore was determined to split their vote and allow the Democrats to win. Or, some contended, he wanted an O'Dwyer victory because he was sure the Democrats would have an ineffective administration that by contrast would make his mayoral years look better. Morris's entry into the race added a wild card that caused problems for the fusion movement, which was bitterly divided over this contest and therefore weakened.

O'Dwyer won a strong victory, taking 57 percent of the vote to Goldstein's 21.9 percent and Morris's 20.8 percent. Morris captured a number of Republican votes and probably would have been a more formidable candidate on the Republican-Liberal-City Fusion line. His defeat and O'Dwyer's election signified the collapse of the fusion movement in New York. Indeed it was the split of the fusion forces that put the Democrats back into power. Certainly La Guardia could have done more to maintain a fusion organization and pick an heir who could have continued his reform effort, but he did not think in terms of an heir. As he had stated, "In a democracy a public official cannot designate his crown prince." It is one of La Guardia's great failings that he, who enjoyed being the center of attention, was reluctant to give the spotlight to anyone else.

A New Tammany?

After La Guardia's reelection in 1937, some of his supporters in a victory parade carried a coffin labeled "Tammany Rests in Pieces." The statement was clearly premature, as O'Dwyer's administration was to show. Seabury made a better prediction in the 1945 campaign when he said that a Democratic or Republican win would bring a 1920s-style corrupt government back to the city. Within a few years, after O'Dwyer's 1949 reelection, various scandals involving corruption and the influence of crime figures in the city

government and Tammany were revealed. O'Dwyer resigned under a cloud in 1950.

What was clear by the time O'Dwyer won the mayoralty
in 1945, and was illustrated by the corruption that followed, was that Tammany had in some ways reverted to the
corrupt Walker days. However, in other ways, mainly because of La Guardia and Roosevelt, the organization had
changed, although not always for the better. As noted earlier, La Guardia's championing of Italian political aspirations had forced the Irish Democratic leaders to try to woo
this group with various positions, although they kept control of the party for themselves. However, by La Guardia's
second term the Italians were capturing more of the
decision-making district leadership positions. Among New
York's Democratic machines, Tammany was the most prone
to pressure. Their self-destructive opposition to Roosevelt
and Lehman in the early 1930s had cost them federal and
state positions. Added to their problems was the forfeiture
of civil service and appointed court posts during La Guardia's twelve-year reign. Additionally, in his reorganization
of city government, the mayor had eliminated a number of
positions that had been Tammany sinecures. Patronage
had provided workers for the party, and court appointments had provided income both from the sale of judgeships and from protection for criminal elements.

Tammany's weakened status opened the way for wealthy
criminal elements to gain control of the machine. Particularly important were some Italian gangsters who used their
wealth and power to advance their group in the Democratic organization. A tie between politics and crime was
not new. Tammany had long been involved in offering protection in return for a fee. As a result, the gangs did not
have to worry about the law, and a number of Tammany
district leaders, mostly Irish, amassed sums that far ex-
ceeded their salaries. The Seabury investigations had earlier revealed some of these connections.

However, the Tammany-criminal connection was soon to change. Salvatore (Charles "Lucky" Luciano) Lucania, the leader of the city's underworld and close ally to various Italian and Jewish gangsters, decided in 1931 to end his relationship with one of the Irish district leaders he had worked with and put an Italian into that position. It is difficult to say what motivated Luciano. It may have been ethnic pride or simply the need to put in someone who was personally loyal to him. Luciano backed Albert Marinelli for the district leader's position of Manhattan's Second Assembly District West, which was then in the hands of Harry Perry, an influential figure among Tammany's ruling Irish. As one knowledgeable political analyst noted, the Italian replacement of the Irish took place in this district after Luciano sent some of his men to "persuade" Perry to step down. Marinelli was then able to become the first Italian district leader in Manhattan and eventually became an influential figure in the Tammany machine.

An increasing gangster influence in politics came at the same time as the already noted Italian desire for more influence in the Democratic party. It also occurred as the La Guardia-inspired pressure pushed the Democrats into making more Italian appointments in order to win the votes of this group. Thus, other Italians moved into district leader positions but without criminal support. However, Marinelli was the only Italian who was able to oust an Irish district leader.

Luciano was only the beginning. The end of his control in 1936, after being successfully prosecuted by Thomas Dewey (later Manhattan district attorney, New York governor, and Republican presidential candidate), led to the emergence of Francesco (Frank Costello) Castiglia as the power behind Tammany. A number of top gangsters were imprisoned, and the political connections between various Tammany district leaders, such as Marinelli and James J. Hines, and the underworld were revealed. Already reeling from La Guardia's reforms, Tammany became desperately short of money. Frank Costello not only replaced Luciano as the dominant criminal leader in the city, but soon became the money power shoring up Tammany. Despite all their efforts, Dewey and La Guardia were never able to seriously damage the organized crime operations in the city or to break the criminal-political connections. The crime business simply went on, and new leaders replaced those who were arrested. At first, Costello had run his operations the usual way, by buying protection. But he soon decided that he would prefer to select and control the district leaders, rather than just buy them off. He often used intimidation to put his own supporters into these positions. Costello's financial resources, violent threats, and control over some district leaders enabled him to exert a significant influence over the Tammany executive committee by 1941. In 1942 he helped to remove the reigning Tammany leader, Christopher Sullivan, and replace him with Michael J. Kennedy. As Kennedy assumed the leadership role of Tammany, so did Costello.

The extent of Costello's power was revealed in 1943, when a wiretap on his phone disclosed a conversation with Thomas Aurelio, a city magistrate who had been chosen as a state supreme court candidate. Aurelio thanked Costello for his efforts in getting the nomination and pledged loyalty to the underworld leader. Costello responded that "when I tell you something is in the bag, you can rest assured." Costello had indeed been the main factor in securing Aurelio's designation as the candidate. Tammany boss Kennedy had thought of choosing an Irishman recommended by Roosevelt instead of an Italian. But Costello pressured Kennedy into giving the nomination to Aurelio, the gangster's choice. When the Costello-Aurelio discussion was revealed, Kennedy disassociated himself from Aurelio. Costello, incensed at Kennedy's action, helped to remove Kennedy in 1943 and replace him with Edward Loughlin as Tammany boss.

Costello remained a powerful figure in Tammany through the 1940s and maintained close ties with the men who officially ran the organization. His influence was felt in the entry of more Italians into district leaderships and judgeships and in the diminishing of the long-held power of the Irish in Tammany. Very often Italians who desired a political career turned to Costello for aid. As noted, however, it was not only gangster influence that led to more political positions for Italians. The Democrats wanted to win this group away from La Guardia and therefore offered it increased opportunities. Additionally, Roosevelt, especially after his 1940 "stab-in-the-back" speech, was interested in wooing the Italian vote and therefore was willing to offer federal patronage.

By the time O'Dwyer was elected in 1945, Tammany had made room for the Italians and other groups (the first black Tammany district leader, Herbert L. Bruce of the Twenty-first Assembly District, was elected in 1935). By 1949, an Italian, Carmine DeSapio, led the political machine. He also was leader of what was known as the Italian bloc among the district leaders. This bloc, with ties to Costello, also included Jews and represented the full emergence of both ethnic groups into leadership roles in Tammany. Their fight was with the Irish, and by the late 1940s the Italians and Jews had won. Hugo Rogers in 1948 became the first Jewish Tammany leader and was quickly followed by Desapio. It was, however, also a weaker machine and one that was more under the influence of criminal elements. La Guardia never managed to destroy the organization he hated. However, he was part of the group, along with Roosevelt, Luciano, and Costello, that made it quite different from its heyday of the 1920s.

O'Dwyer worked with a Tammany machine that was

changing ethnically but was also more corrupt than it had
been since the Walker years. As Tammany declined during
the 1930s and early 1940s, the other Democratic machines
gained power, particularly the Flynn machine in the Bronx
and the Kelly machine in Brooklyn, both of which were favored by Roosevelt with patronage and assumed leadership roles in the New York Democratic party. The Bronx
and Brooklyn machines also proved more resistant to ethnic succession, and the Irish largely retained their power.
However, Tammany maintained considerable influence in
New York politics, even during its waning years. The machine temporarily revived and became a power again in the
1950s under DeSapio, although it never regained the influence it had in pre-La Guardia days.

The Last Years

La Guardia left office on January 1, 1946, with few delu-
sions about the complete destruction of Tammany. Although he now stayed out of New York politics, the former
mayor was still very active in other areas. Had Roosevelt
lived, Fiorello may have moved quickly into another political position. FDR had been interested in La Guardia as a
possible Democratic senatorial candidate in the 1946 election. There was no chance of this nomination after the
president died in 1945, and Fiorello lost his influence in
the White House. La Guardia had no party support, although he was certainly still a popular and charismatic
public figure.

His last years were spent as a columnist for a local newspaper, as a radio commentator with his own programs, and
as director-general of the United Nations Relief and Reha-
bilitation Administration (UNRRA), to which President
Truman appointed him in March 1946. As a radio personality, Fiorello spoke out forcefully on many topics of local
and national interest. Unlike his radio broadcasts as mayor,

these programs had private sponsors. However, within a few months he had alienated the magazine sponsor of his national issues program, who accused La Guardia of making rash and careless statements in his attacks on the "interests," including advertisers. La Guardia's contract was terminated. Fiorello was usually one to speak his mind and was prone, at times, to get overly emotional about his causes and misspeak. His work with UNRRA was initially fulfilling, because this agency provided food and other aid to war-destroyed Europe. Thus, he was able to be in the position he enjoyed most—fighting for a cause, protecting and giving help to the unfortunate, and being in the limelight.

It was during his last period as mayor and in his few months in the UNRRA job that the Holocaust and the evils of the Nazi system were made vividly clear to him in a personal way. Fiorello's sister Gemma had stayed in Europe after he came back to the United States to make his mark. She eventually married Herman Gluck, who was Jewish, and settled with him in Budapest. The Nazis put them both in concentration camps during the war, where Herman subsequently died. Gemma claimed that she was spared because the Germans were aware of her brother's importance and planned, at a future time, to perhaps use her in a trade. When released in 1945 with her daughter and infant grandson, Gemma hoped to come to the United States. Fiorello, who saw his sister and niece in 1946 during a tour as UNRRA head, promised to bring them to America. He contacted various government agencies in the United States and overseas to speed up the process of getting his family into the country. Meanwhile, he sent money regularly to assist her. Gemma and her daughter and grandson finally arrived in America in May 1947 after Fiorello secured scarce space for them on a ship owned by a friend.

La Guardia continued as director-general of UNRRA until the organization was phased out of existence in December 1946. This assignment had become particularly frustrating for him. As the cold war became a reality, opposition had mounted in the United States to providing aid to the peoples of the emerging Soviet bloc. Fiorello wanted to help all the people of Europe without regard to politics. He called on the UN in late 1946 to provide emergency food relief for the coming year and rejected a policy of offering food "only to those countries chosen, picked and acceptable to our own government." He urged the American people to realize that "we are not giving aid to governments. We are giving aid to the men, women and children throughout the world who suffered so much during the war. . . . Does the government of the United States intend to adopt a policy which will make innocent men, women and children suffer because of some political situation which makes their Government unacceptable to the United States?" But in the early cold war days a strictly humanitarian-based aid program became politically impossible.

Worn out by his many arduous activities, disgusted and disappointed by the growing American hostility to his non-political approach to worldwide aid, and not feeling well, La Guardia checked into New York's Mt. Sinai Hospital in April 1947 for tests. Released and then put back in the hospital for more tests, he underwent surgery in June and was diagnosed as having pancreatic cancer, although the press was told that he had chronic pancreatitis. Although he was declining fast, La Guardia tried to keep up his broadcasts and writing (he was now working on his autobiography) until the very end. He finally had to give up his radio broadcasting, but he stayed with his writing until he collapsed into a coma in mid-September. La Guardia died of cancer early in the morning of September 20, 1947, at age sixty-four, and New York mourned. A measure of the man, his honesty, and his desire to do good without any concern for financial reward was revealed when his safe-deposit box was opened after his death. His total assets, besides a mortgaged house, amounted to $8,000 in war bonds—a far cry from the fortunes that corrupt politicians amassed at the expense of the city during the Walker and O'Dwyer years.

CHAPTER SIX

La Guardia: His Place in History

Although La Guardia's influence was most strongly felt in New York City, his significance as a progressive and urban reformer transcended the city's boundaries. In New York, Fiorello showed that urban government could function in an honest, well-managed, public-oriented way. By the time he left office, New York had a new charter with a council elected by proportional representation, a city planning commission to guide New York's development, and a more equitable and better-run civil service. He provided the type of city leadership that the good-government elements of an earlier period had desired. In this sense, he was in the mold of such mayors as Samuel Jones of Toledo and Tom Johnson of Cleveland, who ran their cities in the early years of the twentieth century honestly, efficiently, and with an eye toward solving social problems. La Guardia did all this, but on a grander scale. The advent of the New Deal and the willingness of Washington to extend help to the cities during the depression allowed La Guardia, who was on good terms with Roosevelt, to secure the funds for projects about which the earlier reformers could only dream. A new federal-city partnership emerged out of this era, setting the tone for current times.

It was the combination of late-nineteenth- and early twentieth-century good-government and social reform concepts with the activism and pump-priming of the New Deal that made La Guardia a unique figure. He linked the two periods of urban reform, combining the ideas of both generations of reformers. His ties to Seabury on the one hand and Berle on the other illustrate how he connected the nineteenth- and early twentieth-century urban progressives with those of the 1930s New Deal. As such, La Guardia exemplified the modern mayor—or at least what a city leader should be in our times—managing the city efficiently, providing good, honest government, and making use of federal funds to enhance the urban environment. Few mayors have been able to do as well in the job, indicating again his unique position and suggesting that he was far ahead of his time.

La Guardia also epitomized a new liberalism, which emphasized, not the laissez-faire Jeffersonian liberal views of the nineteenth century, but the activist governmental role of the twentieth century. The new liberalism of the progressives, which called for an involved government that dealt with economic and social problems, found one of its strongest proponents in La Guardia. He was very much a Teddy Roosevelt or Robert La Follette progressive who believed that society could be improved through government intervention. As a congressman he supported social justice through government action. As a mayor, he ran his city with these concepts in mind and showed how much could be done with proper funding. One can see a direct connection among the La Follette/Teddy Roosevelt Progressive era, the La Guardia/Franklin Roosevelt New Deal period, and the Kennedy-New-Frontier/Johnson Great-Society-days of the 1960s. Fiorello was a link in the liberal chain of the twentieth century. Reformers from all three generations recognized a country at risk because of numerous economic, political, and social problems and resolved to work to improve American society.

It is true, as historians such as Richard Hofstadter have

pointed out, that there were differences between the New Deal and the earlier Progressive period. The Progressive movement took place during a time of economic prosperity following a serious depression, whereas the New Deal occurred in the depths of an economic collapse. Yet in all three periods (including that of Kennedy-Johnson), there was a sense of a nation in trouble and of mounting problems that threatened to rend the social fabric. While not all progressives viewed the New Deal as a natural continuation of the earlier attempt to deal with society's problems through strong government action, La Guardia certainly did. He emerged not only as the initial voice of the New Deal in Congress, but as its leading advocate in the cities. Whether in Congress or City Hall, La Guardia was an activist who needed only a sympathetic federal government to fulfill his plans for a just society. Although in subsequent decades the federal government did not always acknowledge its urban responsibilities, the New York mayors who came after Fiorello were not able to ignore the issues he had raised. Welfare, the construction of schools and hospitals, and the development of low-income housing all remained important concerns.

In addition to being a symbol of progressivism and urban reform, La Guardia represented other factors in a changing America. He was, as biographer Arthur Mann and others have pointed out, a marginal man caught between different cultures. He was native-born and was raised in the rural West, but he came to symbolize the rise of the new immigrant groups and the big city. He had Italian and Jewish roots and strong ties to European culture, but he was also a product of the American frontier. In this sense, he was part of an old rural America and a new urban United States, of the native-born Protestant majority (he was raised as an Episcopalian) and the newer Catholic and Jewish immigrants. That he could be all of these things made La Guardia an unusual figure in American politics.

In some ways, therefore, one can categorize him with Al Smith, Robert Wagner and Salvatore Cotillo as an ethnic and a reform leader. But Smith was a born-and-bred New Yorker, of very poor beginnings, who belonged to an older immigrant group. Wagner and Cotillo were foreign-born, and did not come to America until they were nine and ten, respectively. All three went into the Tammany organization, which precluded any strong ties to the anti-Tammany good-government elements. None had much in common with the western progressives. Smith also had little in common with the New Dealers. Although he supported certain social reforms, he objected to the increasing power of the federal government. Combining the appeal and attributes of various reformers, La Guardia was Smith, Wagner, Cotillo, La Follette, and Seabury rolled into one.

Unlike any other politician except Franklin Roosevelt, La Guardia could appeal strongly to both the urban and rural poor and connect the aspirations of both urban and rural reformers. He did not have the liability of appearing to be a provincial New Yorker, like Al Smith. Although he was identified with the city and with the ethnics, Fiorello could point to his Arizona and Protestant background. He was a skillful urban politician but not a Tammany man. He was a New Deal supporter but also a Republican. He crossed ethnic, political, and generational barriers that most others could not. He spoke for the rising Italian population in New York and through his political club and mayoral reforms helped to bring this group into the political mainstream. La Guardia's influence can be seen, for example, in the emergence of his protégé, Vito Marcantonio, as a political power in the city. Voters of Italian descent, whether immigrants or native-born, flocked to Fiorello. He provided respect and status for the immigrant generation and political access and a role model for the younger group. He also furnished political access over a longer time for Seabury and the good-government forces than they had ever had before. A three-term reform fusion administration was unprecedented.

On the political stump and in Congress, La Guardia was a dynamic speaker who was filled with the anger and resentment felt by the abused and downtrodden, and who championed the causes of the underprivileged and powerless. He saw their problems in personal terms, and he fought for a better life for these people while at the same time furthering his own career. Belief and ambition thus often merged to motivate this aggressive advocate for the oppressed. The one piece of major legislation that bears his name, the Norris-La Guardia Act, which protects a worker's right to strike unhampered by the courts and acknowledges the right to form unions and engage in collective bargaining, illustrates his concern. He represented, however, not only the urban industrial class, but also farmers, miners, the aged, and children. Fiorello was angered by how the irresponsible and uncaring wealthy industrial and political leaders treated the less fortunate and less powerful in society and became the protector of the weaker groups.

La Guardia was at his best and his worst when dealing with ethnic issues. In Congress he defended immigrants against nativistic attacks and waged a long fight against laws restricting immigration. He was in the forefront of those public officials who condemned the Nazi regime. However, along with his political opponents, La Guardia manipulated ethnic issues to win votes. A clever, ambitious politician who could speak to his constituents in several languages, Fiorello rode to victory on a number of occasions with ethnic appeals. His campaigns and those of his opponents often revealed the strength of tribal loyalties and at times served to further divide already competing and contentious ethnic groups. But this was the way campaigns were waged in America's multiethnic cities. To La Guardia's credit he usually was not the first to raise the ethnic issue but was always the one to use it to best advantage. In many ways he represented the best in American pluralism; patriotic but also proud of his immigrant heritage, he proved that an ethnic leader and a symbol of the newest citizens could also be solidly American. Along with Smith and Wagner, he provided an effective counterforce to the fears that arose during World War I about dual loyalty.

On racial issues, the mayor was part of a liberal group that generally was ahead of its time. He supported equality and economic opportunities for blacks. But La Guardia saw education and minority self-improvement as the vehicles for changing society. He envisioned blacks improving their lives and achieving acceptance much as the Irish, Italians, and Jews had. He did not seem at first to fully understand how deep rooted racism was in the nation and that it would require different solutions and methods. During World War II, however, as racist employment practices became one of his concerns, he began to recognize the need for stronger government action. His failure to follow his egalitarian beliefs during the Stuyvesant Town controversy and his response to the internment and resettlement of Japanese-Americans were serious shortcomings and illustrated that even racial liberals had far to go before all their actions caught up with all their words. However, life for New York's black citizens did improve under La Guardia.

Today, La Guardia is spoken of and remembered in various ways: from the humorous (rushing to fires and reading the Sunday comic strips over the radio) to the serious (the Norris-La Guardia Act and the battles with Tammany). Arthur Mann describes him as an outsider and a fighter, and he is certainly remembered as both. He was a Republican in a city dominated by Democrats, a progressive congressman in a conservative Congress, an ethnic leader during a xenophobic decade, a New Dealer before the New Deal, a reform mayor in a city long controlled by a political machine, and a well-known Italian-American during a time when the United States was at war with Italy. Even when La Guardia's political philosophies came into vogue under Franklin D. Roosevelt's Democratic party, he remained a Republican or attached himself to various third parties.

La Guardia is best remembered for his mayoral years and his efforts to provide New York with a good, effective and caring government. Thomas Kessner, one of his biographers, writes that "New Yorkers considered him, on balance, not merely a good but a spectacularly great mayor." Seabury, speaking at a radio memorial service for the mayor, stated, "No man who has ever been mayor of New York City did more for its people than Mayor La Guardia. He did not spare himself. His boundless energy was always in action to promote the welfare and happiness of the whole people of New York. . . . Few cities have ever been favored with such a dynamic personality." One can easily agree with these statements. Although La Guardia's strong emotions and intense ambitions sometimes led him astray, he was still an exemplary mayor and a leading reform and ethnic figure who fought valiantly over many years to create an honest, responsive city government, improve the lives of the common people, and provide representation for the new immigrant groups.

BIBLIOGRAPHICAL ESSAY

La Guardia was involved in many events of his time, and information on him can be found in a wide variety of collections and histories. There are several archives that house his papers. The New York Municipal Archives contain primarily his mayoral papers, but also has material predating his mayoralty. Included here are correspondence, investigatory reports, and campaign material going back to his early congressional and World War I service. The New York Public Library manuscript division has correspondence, press releases, scrapbooks, and speeches from La Guardia's congressional and mayoral years. The La Guardia Archives at La Guardia Community College holds Fiorello's personal papers, various speeches, correspondence and records of relatives and associates, such as his sister and wife, oral histories from such figures as Robert Moses and Marie La Guardia, scrapbooks, newsreels, and La Guardia's files as head of UNRRA. Supplementing this material are correspondence with Fiorello and/or references to La Guardia or New York politics in such collections as the Franklin D. Roosevelt papers and Adolf Berle papers (Franklin D. Roosevelt Library, Hyde Park, New York); the Charles C. Burlingham papers (Harvard University Law School Library); the Herbert H. Lehman papers (Columbia University); the Vito Marcantonio papers (New York Public Library); the Robert Moses papers (New York Public Library); and the NAACP papers (Library of Congress). Valuable information can also be found in the oral history collection at Columbia University, which includes interview transcripts with such individuals as William O'Dwyer, Charles C. Burlingham, Paul Windels, Jeremiah Mahoney, Stanley Isaacs, Marie La Guardia, and Herbert Lehman.

Various La Guardia opponents, allies, officials, and relatives have written memoirs that provide information on Fiorello and his times. Among them are: Newbold Morris in collaboration with Dana Lee Thomas, *Let the Chips Fall: My Battles Against Corruption* (New York, 1955); Henry H. Curran, *Pillar to Post* (New York, 1941); Robert Moses, *La Guardia: A Salute and A Memoir* (New York, 1957); Ernest Cuneo, *Life With Fiorello: A Memoir* (New York, 1955); Gemma La Guardia Gluck, *My Story* (New York, 1961); James Farley, *Jim Farley's Story: The Roosevelt Years* (New York, 1948); and Edward Flynn, *You're the Boss* (New York, 1957). Of special note is La Guardia's own unfinished autobiography, which he was still working on at the time of his death, *The Making Of An Insurgent: An Autobiography* (1948, reprint ed. New York, 1961).

The secondary literature on La Guardia consists of a number of biographies, plus material on the mayor included in various works on related topics and individuals. The most useful biographies for my study, and ones that greatly helped me understand Fiorello, were Arthur Mann's two volumes, *La Guardia: A Fighter Against His Times 1882–1933* (Philadelphia, 1959) and *La Guardia Comes to Power, 1933* (Philadelphia, 1965), which ends as La Guardia enters the mayor's office; and Thomas Kessner, *Fiorello H. La Guardia and the Making of Modern New York* (New York, 1989), which covers his entire life. As the title of his first volume suggests, Mann sees Fiorello as being out of step with much of his times, as initially fighting against the major trends of the pre–New Deal era. By supporting pluralism and social reform and rejecting nativism, the Tammany machine, policies that favored the rich, and socialist panaceas, La Guardia emerges as an ambitious and skillful insurgent and reformer who also cared deeply about those he represented. Mann also raises the point (as does Howard Zinn in his study of La Guardia's congressional career, from which I also benefited, *La Guardia in Congress* [Ithaca, N.Y., 1959]) that La Guardia was a New Dealer before the New Deal and tied together the Progressive and New Deal reform eras. The progressive as New Dealer is a theme about which historians have written much. There was no easy movement from one reform thrust to the other. Not all reformers who had supported Theodore Roosevelt's or Woodrow Wilson's programs backed the New Deal. Many emerged as critics. La Guardia's commitment to the poor, his belief in a strong, positive government that supported social reform, and his defense of immigrants and unions put him, as Mann and Zinn first note, in the New Deal camp early, even anticipating the 1930s reforms.

Studies of other progressives should be consulted as well to understand any Progressive–New Deal connections. See, for example, Richard Lowitt, *George W. Norris, the Persistence of a Progressive* (Urbana, Ill., 1971), and his *George W. Norris: The Triumph of a Progressive* (Urbana, Ill., 1978), as well as LeRoy Ashby, *The Spearless Leader, Senator Borah and the Progressive Movement in the 1920s* (Urbana, Ill., 1972), and David Thelan, *Robert M. La Follette and the Insurgent Spirit* (Boston, 1976). Also see Richard Hofstadter's *The Age of Reform* (New York, 1955), and particularly consult John D. Buenker, *Urban Liberalism and Progressive Reform* (New York, 1973), for good general discussions of the ties between progressivism and the New Deal and the role of the urban middle class and poor in the reform movements. The place of the political machine and lower-class immigrant-stock politicians in the reforms of the Progressive movement and New Deal is ably noted in J. Joseph Huthmacher's "Urban Liberalism and the Age of Reform," *Mississippi Valley Historical Review* 44 (September 1962): 321–41, and especially in his *Senator Robert F. Wagner and the Rise of Urban Liberalism* (New York, 1968). Wagner, like La Guar-

dia, represented the ethnic poor and served as a link between the Progressive and New Deal eras. But Wagner was
also a Tammany man. On Tammany and reform, see also
Thomas Henderson, "Immigrant Politician: Salvatore Cotillo, Progressive Ethnic," *International Migration Review* 13
(Spring 1979): 81–102, and his *Tammany Hall and the New
Immigrants: The Progressive Years* (New York, 1976); also con-
sult Nancy Joan Weiss, *Charles Francis Murphy, 1858–1924:
Respectability and Responsibility in Tammany Politics* (North-
ampton, Mass., 1968); Paula Eldot, *Alfred E. Smith: The Pol-
itician as Reformer* (New York, 1983); Steven P. Erie,
*Rainbow's End: Irish-Americans and the Dilemmas of Machine
Politics, 1840–1985* (Berkeley, 1988); and for an analysis of
Democratic party politics in the 1920s, David Burner, *The
Politics of Provincialism: The Democratic Party in Transition,
1918–1932* (New York, 1967).

Although Kessner's book reveals La Guardia's New Deal
connections as well, his main theme is that Fiorello was a
pioneer in establishing a close relationship between city
government and federal government that presaged the ties
between the two in the modern era. In a well written and
thoroughly researched study, Kessner, although much
more critical of La Guardia than were Mann and Zinn in
their biographies (which do not cover the mayoral years), is
able to portray Fiorello in his proper historical role as an
urban leader and innovator.

Other biographies that were useful but generally not as
thoroughly researched or analytical included August
Heckscher with Phyllis Robinson, *When La Guardia Was
Mayor: New York's Legendary Years* (New York, 1978); Lowell
M. Limpus and Burr W. Leyson, *This Man La Guardia* (New
York, 1938); William Manners, *Patience and Fortitude: Fior-
ello La Guardia* (New York, 1976); Lawrence Elliott, *Little
Flower: The Life and Times of Fiorello La Guardia* (New York,
1983); and Jay Franklin, *La Guardia: A Biography* (New

York, 1937). I would further add to this list La Guardia's
Planning Commission chairman Rexford Tugwell's analysis
of Fiorello's career, *The Art of Politics As Practiced By Three
Great Americans: Franklin Delano Roosevelt, Luis Muñoz Ma-
rín, and Fiorello H. La Guardia* (New York, 1958); and Civil
Service Commission president Paul Kern's "Fiorello La
Guardia," in *The American Politician*, ed. J. T. Salter (Chapel
Hill, N.C., 1938). La Guardia's experience in World War I
as a pilot is the focus of Maurer Maurer, "Flying with Fior-
ello: The U.S. Air Service in Italy, 1917–1918," *The Airpower
Historian* 11 (1964): 113–18. His 1929 campaign is covered
in M. R. Werner, "Fiorello's Finest Hour," *American Heritage*
(October 1961): 38–41, 106–11.

The mayoral period is treated well in a number of publications other than those already mentioned. The best book
focusing particularly on La Guardia's tenure as mayor is
Charles Garrett, *The La Guardia Years, Machine and Reform
Politics in New York City* (New Brunswick, N.J., 1961). Garrett
places La Guardia's career within the historical context of
New York's political battles between Tammany and reform.
Other well-done studies of the reform-fusion or mayoral
period include William P. Brown, "The Political and Administrative Leadership of Fiorello H. La Guardia as
Mayor of the City of New York, 1934–1941," vol. 1, and "An
Administrative Study of Some Aspects of the 1934–1941
Mayoralty of Fiorello H. La Guardia," vol. 2 (Ph.D. dissertation, New York University, 1959–1960). Brown delves
into events, such as transit unification, that illustrate the
mayor's innovative leadership and the benefits New York
derived from his administration. Other worthwhile studies
of this period include Leonard Chalmers, "The Crucial
Test of La Guardia's First Hundred Days: The Emergency
Economy Bill," *New York Historical Society Quarterly* 57 (July
1973): 237–53, which describes La Guardia's political skills
in the early days of his mayoralty; Chalmers, "Fiorello La

Guardia, Paterfamilias at City Hall: An Appraisal," *New York History* 56 (April 1975): 211–25, which discusses Fiorello's personality, work ethic, and style of governing; and Gerard Davis, "The Success of Fusion Reform in 1933" (Ph.D. dissertation, Columbia University, 1977), a careful analysis of the fusion coalition that supported La Guardia. For an understanding of New York politics also consult Alfred Connable and Edward Silberfarb, *Tigers of Tammany* (New York, 1967); Warren Moscow, *Politics in the Empire State* (New York, 1948); Moscow, *What Have You Done for Me Lately? The Ins and Outs of New York City Politics* (Englewood, N.J., 1967); Moscow, *The Last of the Big-Time Bosses: The Life and Times of Carmine De Sapio and the Rise and Fall of Tammany Hall* (New York, 1971); Theodore Lowi's *At the Pleasure of the Mayor: Patronage and Power in New York City, 1898–1958* (New York, 1964), which discusses mayoral appointments; Wallace Sayre and Herbert Kaufman, *Governing New York: Politics in the Metropolis* (New York, 1960); and on crime, Alan A. Block, "Lepke, Kid Twist and the Combination: Organized Crime in New York City, 1930–1944" (Ph.D. dissertation, UCLA, 1975); and Jenna Weissman Joselit, *Our Gang: Jewish Crime and the New York Jewish Community, 1900–1940* (Bloomington, Ind., 1983).

La Guardia's attitude toward unions and strikes is covered best in George Kaplan, "The Labor Views of Fiorello H. La Guardia" (Ph.D. dissertation, New York University, 1962), which analyzes the development of his thoughts through his congressional and mayoral years.

The relief issue is ably treated in Joseph Verdicchio, "New Deal Work Relief and New York City: 1933–1938" (Ph.D. dissertation, New York University, 1980); Barbara Blumberg, *The New Deal and the Unemployed: The View from New York City* (Lewisburg, Pa., 1979); and Dominic F. O'Keefe, "The History of Home Relief in New York City 1938 through 1967" (Ph.D. dissertation, New York University, 1978).

La Guardia as a voice of the new ethnics is covered in Ronald H. Bayor's *Neighbors in Conflict: The Irish, Germans, Jews, and Italians of New York City, 1929–1941* (1978; 2nd ed., Urbana, Ill., 1988), which deals with La Guardia's involvement in the ethnic political succession, intergroup conflicts, and foreign events of the 1930s and early 1940s, and also analyzes Fiorello's mayoral votes by ethnicity. A study that also addresses the issue of the mayor's response to Nazi Germany's anti-Semitism is David M. Esposito and Jackie R. Esposito, "La Guardia and the Nazis, 1933–1938," *American Jewish History* 78 (September 1988): 38–53. For background on the large ethnic communities in New York, see Moses Rischin, *The Promised City: New York's Jews, 1870–1914* (Cambridge, Mass., 1962); Irving Howe, *World of Our Fathers* (New York, 1976); Deborah Dash Moore, *At Home in America: Second Generation New York Jews* (New York, 1981); George E. Pozzetta, "The Italians of New York City, 1890–1914" (Ph.D. dissertation, University of North Carolina, Chapel Hill, 1971); and Donna Gabaccia, *From Sicily to Elizabeth Street: Housing and Social Change Among Italian Immigrants, 1880–1930* (Albany, N.Y., 1984). On the political organization of the Italian community, besides Henderson and Bayor, see Philip V. Cannistraro, "Generoso Pope and the Rise of Italian-American Politics, 1925–1936," in *Italian Americans: New Perspectives in Italian Immigration and Ethnicity*, ed. Lydio Tomasi (New York, 1985).

Fiorello also was deeply involved with New York's black community. The leading scholar of this interaction is Dominic Capeci, who has written a number of carefully researched studies, including "From Different Liberal Perspectives: Fiorello H. La Guardia, Adam Clayton Powell, Jr., and Civil Rights in New York City, 1941–1943," *Journal of Negro History* 62 (1977): 160–73; *The Harlem Riot of 1943* (Philadelphia, 1977); "Fiorello H. La Guardia and the Stuyvesant Town Controversy of 1943," *New York Historical Society Quarterly* 62 (October 1978): 289–310; "Fiorello H.

La Guardia and the American Dream: A Document," *Italian Americana* 4 (1978): 1–21; "Walter F. White and the Savoy Ballroom Controversy of 1943," *Afro-Americans in New York Life and History* 5 (July 1981): 13–32; and "Fiorello H. La Guardia and Employment Discrimination, 1941–1943," *Italian Americana* 9 (1983): 49–67. Other studies shed light on Harlem in this period or on the problems which the black community faced. Of particular importance is Larry A. Greene, "Harlem in the Great Depression, 1928–1936" (Ph.D. dissertation, Columbia University, 1979); Thomas Henderson, "Harlem Confronts the Machine: The Struggle for Local Autonomy and Black District Leadership," *Afro-Americans in New York Life and History* 3 (1979): 51–68; Michael L. Goldstein, "Black Power and the Rise of Bureaucratic Autonomy in New York City Politics: The Case of Harlem Hospital, 1917–1931," *Phylon* 41 (1980): 187–201; Mark Naison, *Communists in Harlem during the Depression* (Urbana, Ill., 1983); and John C. Walter, *The Harlem Fox: J. Raymond Jones and Tammany, 1920–1970* (Albany, N.Y., 1989).

Studies of those who interacted with or were close to Fiorello should be consulted. One cannot understand La Guardia, his career, or New York at this time without also reading analyses of such individuals as Seabury and Marcantonio among others. See, for example, Herbert Mitgang, *The Man Who Rode the Tiger: The Life of Judge Samuel Seabury and the Story of the Greatest Investigation of City Corruption in this Century* (New York, 1963); Gerald J. Meyer, "Vito Marcantonio: A Successful New York City Radical Politician" (Ph.D. dissertation, City University of New York, 1983), published by SUNY Press in 1989 as *Vito Marcantonio: Radical Politician, 1902–1954*; Alan Schaffer, *Vito Marcantonio, Radical in Congress* (Syracuse, N.Y., 1966); Salvatore La Gumina, *Vito Marcantonio: The People's Politician* (Dubuque, Iowa, 1969); Alan Nevins, *Herbert H. Lehman and His Era* (New York, 1963); Robert P. Ingalls, *Herbert H.*

Lehman and New York's Little New Deal (New York, 1975); Jordan A. Schwarz, *Liberal: Adolf A. Berle and the Vision of An American Era* (New York, 1987); Robert Caro, *The Power Broker: Robert Moses and the Fall of New York* (New York, 1974); Gene Fowler, *Beau James: The Life and Times of Jimmy Walker* (New York, 1949); George Walsh, *Gentleman Jimmy Walker: Mayor of the Jazz Age* (New York, 1974).

Books about Franklin Roosevelt, Eleanor Roosevelt, and the New Deal also provide information on La Guardia. See particularly Arthur M. Schlesinger, Jr., *The Age of Roosevelt*, vol. 3: *The Politics of Upheaval, 1935–1936* (Boston, 1960); Joseph Lash, *Eleanor and Franklin* (New York, 1971), which describes Eleanor Roosevelt's and La Guardia's work in the Office of Civilian Defense; and his *Eleanor: The Years Alone* (New York, 1972). For an insider's account of the Roosevelt administration, consult Harold Ickes, *The Secret Diary of Harold Ickes*, 3 vols. (New York, 1953–54). For a good one-volume study of the New Deal that includes some brief mentions of La Guardia, see William E. Leuchtenburg, *Franklin D. Roosevelt and the New Deal* (New York, 1963). Also consult James MacGregor Burns, *Roosevelt: The Lion and the Fox* (New York, 1956); Frank Freidel, *Franklin D. Roosevelt, A Rendezvous with Destiny* (Boston, 1990); Kenneth S. Davis, *FDR, The New York Years, 1928–1933* (New York, 1979); and his *FDR, The New Deal Years, 1933–1937* (New York, 1979).

The American Labor party has been chronicled in Robert F. Carter, "Pressure from the Left: The American Labor Party, 1936–1954" (Ph.D. dissertation, Syracuse University, 1965); and Kenneth Waltzer, "The American Labor Party: Third Party Politics in New Deal–Cold War New York, 1936–1954" (Ph.D. dissertation, Harvard University, 1978).

Quoted passages included in this book have been drawn from primary sources and from the following secondary sources: Garrett, *The La Guardia Years*; Limpus and Leyson,

This Man La Guardia; Brown, "The Political and Administrative Leadership," and "An Administrative Study"; Heckscher, *When La Guardia Was Mayor*; Verdicchio, "New Deal Work Relief"; Chalmers, "The Crucial Test," and "Fiorello La Guardia"; Moscow, *Politics*, and *What Have You Done*, and *Last of Big Time*; Weiss, *Charles Francis Murphy*; Nevins, *Herbert H. Lehman*; Kaplan, "The Labor Views"; Connable and Silberfarb, *Tigers*; Esposito, "La Guardia and the Nazis"; Mitgang, *The Man Who Rode*; Manners, *Patience*; Schwarz, *Liberal*; Burner, *The Politics*; Capeci, "Fiorello H. La Guardia and the American Dream"; and especially Zinn, *La Guardia in Congress*; Mann, *La Guardia: A Fighter* and *La Guardia Comes to Power*; and Kessner, *Fiorello H. La Guardia*.

INDEX

Fiorello La Guardia: Ethnicity and Reform
Copy editor, Anita Samen
Sponsoring editor, Maureen Hewitt
Production editor, Lucy Herz
Typesetter, Graphic Composition, Inc.
Printer, McNaughton & Gunn, Inc.
Book designer, Roger Eggers

About the author: Professor Ronald H. Bayor, born in New York
City, teaches history at Georgia Institute of Technology and is
Editor of the *Journal of American Ethnic History.* Professor Bayor's
other books include *Neighbors in Conflict: The Irish, Germans,
Jews and Italians of New York City, 1929–41; Neighbors in Urban
America;* and *Engineering the New South: Georgia Tech, 1885–1985*
(co-author). He has also authored numerous articles on race and
ethnic relations in American cities.